LOCAL WONDERS

First published in 2021 by
Dedalus Press
13 Moyclare Road
Baldoyle
Dublin D13 K1C2
Ireland

www.dedaluspress.com

ISBN 978-1-910251-88-1 (paperback)
ISBN 978-1-910251-89-8 (hardback)

Dedalus Press titles are available in Ireland
from Argosy Books (www.argosybooks.ie) and in the UK
from Inpress Books (www.inpressbooks.co.uk)

Cover image: Ardea-studio / Shutterstock
Design and typesetting: Pat Boran

The Dedalus Press receives financial assistance from
The Arts Council / An Chomhairle Ealaíon.

LOCAL WONDERS

Poems of our Immediate Surrounds

Edited by Pat Boran

DEDALUS PRESS

Contents

≈

✺

INTRODUCTION

W hat do we love? When troubles and doubts threaten to overwhelm us, what sustains or inspires us? What are the things we cannot do without?

The events of the last eighteen months or so have caused many of us to re-examine the very nature of our lives, to reconsider the value of things that, until recently, we took for granted.

Yet somehow they have also taught us to see the world afresh, leading to new discoveries, both tiny and monumental – and often right on our very doorsteps.

Local Wonders brings together some of the great many poems written all over the island of Ireland, and beyond, since early 2020 – when the world as we know it was so utterly changed. Featuring new and emerging poets as well as more established voices, this book is a record of an extraordinary time. More importantly, though, it is a record of how we have learned to review and adapt, and a re-mapping of our relationship to our immediate surrounds.

Some of us are, of course, luckier than others. Not everyone's 5K travel radius afforded them a vista of mountains and sea. But one of the superpowers of poetry has ever been its ability to shine a light on the near-to-hand so that it takes on new meaning, new significance. In such a light, the small, the fragile or the endangered may prove as brilliant a beacon of hope as the sun and stars themselves.

Here, then, are poems of love and affection, of discovery and re-discovery, of rhythms long established or recently recalled. Here are poems that sing the praises of the outdoors, less concerned with our geographical reach as with the depth of our engagement. Walking, hiking, climbing, swimming, gardening, reading, singing, small-talking, listening to and playing music, sitting quietly, just breathing … Have our parks, beaches, river walks and playing fields or the benches in our town squares ever been more popular or frequented?

As we miss encounters with each other, animals play a more significant role than ever: cats and dogs, as we might expect, but also birds in enormous numbers, not least in their role as messengers from the wild to our more 'civilized' realm, finding us out wherever we are, whatever we are at. Here too are foxes, minke whales, ponies, cows, spiders, even Fungi the Dolphin who, leaving us in 2020, remains a kind of symbol of profound non-verbal communication between another species and ourselves.

Again and again these poems remind us of the importance of acceptance, of biding our time, of 'going with the flow'. From Ben Keatinge's observation of a surfer at Doonloughan ('a one-man show flung perfectly to shore') to Martina Dalton's mantra on a walk through a saltmarsh at midnight *('Empty yourself,* it says – *to fill with light'),* there are lessons to be learned from the simple act of paying attention.

Nor is it all about learning to cope on our own. Trish Bennett's portrait of a mother-and-daughter's improvised girl band ('crank it up to the MAX, sing and dance – no matter what') resists the pervasive gloom with a kind of barbaric yawp. While in Ivy Bannister's portrait of two friends, out at last together for a drive at the end of lockdown, we see the friend become 'herself at the wheel, radiant / as an angel'. It is a transformation that many of us will recognise, and one that comes less from the changes that have taken place in the world as in our way of seeing it. As ever, poems ask us not just to look, but to look again, to look deeper. Observation first, ideas afterwards.

And in looking again, attentively, over and over we find the familiar remade. The streets of Chandrika Narayanan-Mohan's Dublin 8 have about them 'a cutlery-clink dinnertime hush'. Katie Martin's statue of Daniel O'Connell 'descends from his granite plinth / to inspect the bullet holes in Courage's chest'. Poems of transformation and wonder are filed like newspaper reports from the coast of Antrim, a standing stone off the R697, the sally bushes of Lough Corrib and the back roads of the Corca Dhuibhne Gaeltacht; from a barn dance for two, the topmost branches of an apple tree, a trampoline in Missouri and a drive-in movie in Kilbeggan. Holidays in caravans, black humour from a County Cork churchyard, radiant memories of international travel – the past and the present whisper to each other as we struggle to imagine what the future may bring.

As far from sea level as one can get on this island, Marguerite Doyle joins a group climbing Carrauntoohil and leaves 'prayer-rags on outcrops … fluttering after us'. There are many grand claims made for poetry that, I suspect, only get in the way of its natural conversation between poet and reader. But one thing is undoubtedly true: the prayer-rags we leave behind us are the same ones that the next climbers are greeted by as they crest the summit. And that, in fact, is no small thing.

Though born out of personal experience or close observation, the best poems almost always feel like anonymous offerings in a larger, collective exchange – like the finished book left for the next visitor at the local coffee shop, or the plastic dog bowl, magically refilled each day outside the closed-up pub.

In hard times it turns out the solution is not to ignore or withdraw from the world but to learn to focus on the things that nourish us. Memory has a role to play, with its resistance to the passing of time, its reminders of a brighter elsewhere that may net return. But, whatever their subject of interest, the best poems seem to me attentive also to the here-and-now, to the moment of their composition, the landscapes and streetscapes out of which they arise, at times startling messengers from another realm. I'm reminded of Clifton Redmond's touching portrait of his mother threading a needle – first the essential focus on the near-to-hand, then afterwards on 'a world beyond the eye'.

In these still challenging times *Local Wonders* is, above all else, an invitation to name and sing the praises of what is of value to us now – to look intently and see what is there, and then to see beyond into the better world that poetry brings into the light.

— PAT BORAN

The Cypress Poem

Yes, we lost that second cypress to the saw
of an idiot neighbour: an immense squarish one,

paired with ours

like an old couple reaching across an untended wall.

But soon enough

I saw three other smaller cypress above another neighbour's
stone-roofed shed, like slim arrowheads or svelte swords
I had never thought about or dwelt upon. A lesson in itself:
vistas of incremental change after a great clean-cut change.

The Finishing Touch

In the background the town is all there:
castle, church spire, river. The railway bridge
connects to the middleground, where
the shopping centre car park is full
of empty spaces.
The ticket machine operates at a loss.
In the draper's window
the discounted jacket drops its stitches
out of fashion
onto the foreground
of discarded masks and gloves.

You are the watercolour character
on a park bench.

In the sky I paint a bird
who has forgotten how to fly.

In the Car with Margaret

At last, our faces masked, we're
in her car again, two persons
from different households
on a jaunt to buy organic veg,
and the breeze that blasts
through open windows
stirs everything to life,
all movement and light.
Lord, to think of the past
when we sped off to garden
or gallery, and gossiped
keenly, souls not awake
to the joy of this world,
flecks of colour everywhere.
Now a painting unfurls
around us – my white shirt,
herself at the wheel, radiant
as an angel, hair bobbed,
the orange ring in flower
on her finger, the scarf
that she's dyed
brighter than the Aegean.

Every start is weak

Still only, ever only, Tuesday. Am in charge
of a cat curled up out in the rain. Tie-dye cat,
quite manky and vegan, except for corn-fed,
free-range Shannonvale capon, served on a bed
of Kerguelen cabbage and cloudberries. If you
can get them, note said. Cash is on countertop.
And, no reason, but through the rain – luscious, hopeless –
salient rose the *seanrá* I'd found, an old saying
I had jotted down from *Dúchas ponc* I E.
Down all the list, many notable sayings, *seanráite,*
it was this *seanrá* stuck and salient rose, the second
Tuesday of rain, minding the cat. May it stay
with you as it stays with me. Every start is weak.

Clare Island, March 2020

> *No man is an island entire of itself; every man*
> *is a piece of the continent, a part of the main;*
> *if a clod be washed away by the sea …*
> *— John Donne*

Isolation is a word that tastes like snow
but it is spring, and so the lambs are born.
Lamb after dead lamb, wrung from the wet ground.
You lift them, your face twisted with bitten rage
at death and what you could have done. The elements
are all conspiring: wet, disease, cold.

Within on the island, we say:
No one, nothing non-essential should come in here
but still the boat goes and comes back again with us
and what and who we need or want.
Isolation melts on our tongues; our hands
intrinsically reach for each other,
and so, some of us will die.

When the weather turns good again, we will look back
and say: That was a dark time. What we could have done,
what we should have known. But everything was against us.
Our own love was a poison more deadly than being alone.

Corona Calypso

The daughter – in charge of the playlist,
cranked Harry Belafonte up to MAX.
Harry lifted us off the couch and onto our feet.

As we started to do interpretative dance
the dog joined our conniptions,
barking and biting our arses.

Parrot – a Harry fan,
went buck-mad for calypso,
got onto his outside swing to be swung,

whistled upside down to *Matilda,*
lay on his back in my hand
to be coochie-cooed.

I coochie-cooed,
he coochie-cooed back –
it was all too much for the cat.

The daughter hoked in her box of stuff
to find her rattling-egg.
I threw beer-bottle caps into a ziplock bag

and we sang as loud as we could
while she rattled her egg,
I shook my cap-tambourine to the beat,

Angelina, Matilda and *Banana Boat*
on REPEAT for Parrot,
who whistled along

until he started to nip
and had to be put in
to calm down.

When she's grown-up and gone
to a home of her own,
I hope the daughter remembers

what to do when times are tough,
crank it up to MAX, sing and dance
– no matter what.

My Post Lives the Life of my Dreams

I love to track from dispatch,
watch it travel to everywhere we're not allowed go.

The daughter's iPad cover
sailed across the Irish sea on the Princess Royal DC.

A sleeveless jacket I bought for Himself in the shed,
winged its way over from Hinchley.

Even though his big birthday in Paris was cancelled,
the present of throwing knives flew from Russia

to be stuck in a warehouse in Portadown for a week.
These days – even that's exotic.

My North Circular Summer Odyssey

Friday evening, three things. The first:
the supermarket's self-checkout, where I swipe
the codes on nets of limes and lemons, ripe
tomatoes, bags of rocket, items reversed

to the scan, whose ruby strobe lasers each
in the wave of things, and tolls an austere disco
of dull beeps. I see, beyond low windows,
the sky inflame like a stretch of hot beach.

And my heart! The machine now hooping green to red
as BOP BOP BOP cries the Pražský, irregular.
Assistance needed. I pause, waiting for the worker,
the can in hand, and in the little mirror overhead

there peep my eyes above my mask's blue stretch
lens-cool and camera-green.
                                        Second thing:
as I lump home, and Drumalee unstrings
dark brick and terraced row, on chairs and ledges

sit the neighbours, hanging out their fronts
abuzz with drink, oozing laughter lustrous-
ly, blasting beats upwards to buttress
orange dusk, pulsing obelisks of OONTZ OONTZ OONTZ –

I stare over. A man pumps up his fist
in the air towards me, I pump mine back,
he cheers, all woop, then stop, as hooves clack
slow of a Garda's horse, the air by his hi-vis

yellowed.

        And last: so drunk these stars that glue
the night to water, the Royal Canal spills
out diamonds. We laugh and laugh and laugh until
WEEEE-OOH, WEEEE-OOH; a car approaches, flashing blue.

Mindful

Take it back to the earliest moment,
to the point where a bud breaks the earth
before stretching yellow into daffodils,

back to the grains of sun-dried sand
before the white rim of waves wash ashore,
back to the slightest turn as whooper swans

circle overhead, flowing homewards,
to the pause when a wild rabbit sees you
watching him, before he scarpers into hiding,

back to the early notes of a Springsteen song,
to the smell of coffee beans on opening a bag,
to a paint-full brush touching blank canvas,

take it to raindrops and sunlight as a rainbow
appears, to a Harvest moon before cloud drift,
to a memory that sparks before a story is told,

to that first moment a child says your name,
to a thought that takes hold before a poem
unfolds, to a bowed head before a prayer.
Take it back to the earliest moment. Breathe.

Eden Terrace

for my son, Diarmuid

While no Champs-Élysées, Ramblas or Alexanderplatz,
Surely this tiny cul-de-sac deserves a laudatory verse.
Hidden by steep steps that prevent vehicular access,

Its quartet of small single-storey cottages face each other.
A square so unobtrusively concealed for twelve decades
That passers-by are rarely ever aware of its existence,

Or how a boy longed to live here for its magical address
Or harsh winters when arrivals found its name an apt choice,
Shelter seekers climbing its steps to glimpse a view of paradise.

Iveagh Gardens

I am eating sweet cherries, throwing
stones into the flower beds. The roses
have petalled the earth as if a body
has crossed East Coast Road en route
to Besant Nagar cremation ground.

The cherries are juicy. The magpies
gather between rose beds. The pigeons
coo childhood summers to me. Lovers
sit on other benches. They do not kiss.
One rose is still perfect. The bush holds it high.

The cherries shine in my hand. The parents
call their kids back from the rocky hill.
The man calls his dog. The vodka drinker
has taken his argument elsewhere.

I leave some cherries uneaten. I want
to share the joy of juice and sweetness,
this half-empty bench, this rose garden
with its petals dying into the soil.

BUILDING THE ARK

As a boy every time it rained for long enough
I used to wonder if the time had come
to take up tools and venture out
into my father's shed
to build the ark.

How real, how heartfelt
something in that Bible story was –
old Noah, in terror of destruction,
for days and nights on end
down on his knees, the waters
rising in all directions;

and those innocent beasts,
hoping they might yet become his friends,
lining up obediently in pairs,
as if that might yet make all the difference,
as if that might help them stand out from the rest.

Something in it struck a chord in me.
I'd gathered frogspawn from a local pool
to watch it hatch, a bowl of punctuation,
but which of all those wriggling glyphs
was I supposed to choose?

I'd stood in awe of older lads
who came, invariably in twos,
long after dark to our back yard,
armed with only flashlights and hessian bags,
scaling the rusted downpipes without a thought
to lamp the hapless pigeons in their roosts.

In the faint light weeping from their bulbs, how did they choose
which to take and breed, and which to loose?

Back then I couldn't walk the full length of the street
but stopped to greet each lonesome dog
that stood by patiently to guard the public space.
I loved the scut, the whelp, the runt
at least as much as any so-called pure-bred pup.
If the choice were mine, I'd populate my ark
from the local pound, with the rescue mutts,
then the one-legged gull from our neighbour's roof,
or the half-blind mule, rough as an unstuffed couch,
that decades back rested its snout
in my palm for a moment —
and has yet to lift it out.

And how did Noah ever resolve
the sleeping arrangements of lions and lambs,
of piranhas, sharks and whales,
or, standing on deck as the packed ark
at last rose off its blocks
to slip out over the waves,
establish the ground rules
for woodpeckers, wood lice, wood worm?

I've loved the story for a lifetime now,
but it seems this best-known version's got it wrong.
It's not that Noah saves the animals
but that the animals, as ever, save the man;

in times of overwhelming fear,
in times of sleeplessness and strife,
the cause that lifts the eye, the mind,
the troubled heart; the point of focus
in the flooded landscape of our lives.

Calculated Risk

The sign over the shop is faded blue
paint flakes of O'Toole or O'Fool
you find in your hair later.

Outside, boxes of headless Barbies
and unreadable Mills and Boons
three for a euro obscure the window.

Ironing boards   clothes horses
deck chairs   golf clubs
half-block the doorway.

Inside, burning patchouli joss sticks
can't obliterate
the smell of unwashed sneakers.

The shopkeepers are volunteers
churchgoing souls who accept
your offering – a black plastic bag –

with grace. It has stagnated
in your spare room for a year
beside the Christmas decorations.

Now you're ready to see the back
of the Trilby Fedora, feathered Panama
and Donegal tweed flat-cap.

You forget to factor in the spectre
of your father walking round the town.

Then Beggars Would Ride

The legends say a butterfly,
if you can speak your dream before it leaves
the kingdom of your gaze,
will carry your caterpillar wish –
a harsh, hairy thing, slow, an ugly flex –
to fruit, and to flower.

A flicker of wings in April,
unseasonal sun at Easter,
and a cabbage white has visited my garden. Its beauty
makes me panic, sets me clamouring for what I wish
today. Is there someone sick, someone I mustn't forget to gift
this winged moment – or can I want, now?

This flashing chance at validation, this light thing
that could bless my dreams, is going, towards the traffic
on Crumlin Road (*you live,* I tell myself,
beside a children's hospital,
wish for cures and comfort, not
cool silvered coins and misting glasses on a table
between the right two beating hearts).

In the face of too much want, nothing screams in time,
before the cabbage white takes
its fleeting chance of grace and shrugs away.
There'll be a first star tonight, or a clock's hands
will join in prayer to catch my wish.
Maybe I'll remember
by nightfall, what I want above all else.

There is no privilege greater
than to have nothing to ask
of a butterfly
but its presence in your garden.

Cinnamon Tea

On the shelves of Belfast's Asian Supermarket
is that cinnamon tea I couldn't find out East,
the only hospitality I could offer,

along with dates dad packed,
5 years ago, when I brought her back
to Maytower, the night we met.

From jungle palms I've called it in,
my rainy forest of fleeting bluebells
and ferns unfurling by the bog-brown burn.

Cherry trees spring pink at the home house
where Dad wraps the hot water bottle
with mum's nightdress, she's an ashy pet,

like my love, who wears thermals in July,
but here we can kiss in lifts, hold hands
in streets, maybe find home in a small town

of abattoirs and assembly lines that I left,
where I put my mum to bed. Here you'll not sit –
wash the curtains cause it's a great day for drying.

I scope the aisles, feedback on the availability
of her comfort food to ease her entry, cook up
our life here, eating edamame, sipping cinnamon tea.

Birdwatcher

for Seán Lysaght

I have lived on this clifftop
For half a century, and yet

Only now, over these last
Few locked-down weeks,

Did I learn to angle a lens
Onto the gaping beaks

And voracious red throats
Of four fledgling ravens

Nested precariously
On a grassy ledge close by.

And I now see how exactly
Flocks of tideline sanderlings

Can anticipate the speed
And reach of shore-waves,

Their precise, scurrying lift
And flutter, the probing beaks

Punctuating every advance
And retreat. And if I live

Long enough I will learn
To recognise how its size,

As well as the long downturn
Of its bill, help to distinguish

The curlew, a threatened species,
From the whimbrel, which is not.

21ˢᵗ April, 2020

A Vision in a Time of Disease

for James Harpur

Perhaps the story will strain belief, but no more
Or less than many others. In any case, one Vita
Relates how a saintly monk was so consumed

By pity for a youth, whose life was blighted
By disease, and who had come to him in search
Of a miracle, that, in search of his own heaven,

The monk took unto himself the youth's infection,
Thus healing him. It further tells that, years later,
With the name of having lived with the disease

In holiness and fortitude in the service of others,
The monk petitioned his abbot for a dispensation
Before his death to make a peregrinatio to Rome

To pray before its sacred relics and gilded altars
And walk among its columns and sunlit squares.
But the abbot, seeing the ravages of the disease

And anticipating how travelling might affect it,
Demurred, forbidding it with the full authority
Of his office. Being, nonetheless, a kindly man

Who saw the consternation his words had caused,
He bade the weeping monk lay his head in his lap.
The monk did so, and when, hours later, he awoke,

What traveller's tales he had brought, from Rome
And from eternity, and from even further abroad!
These he related to the abbot and to all the monks

Who now gathered around, all agog to discover
How he had found, in the lap of here and now,
The only heaven they would ever know, or need.

February 2021

Light Rail

Pre-dawn. Bray Station's
screech and shunt. Morning
is a wet nose and snuffle,
four paws flopping to the floor
for the first excursion. Outside
the street is a neon stage-set –
the first slow train unspooling
its show-reel across a bridge
in a series of stills, the sitters
sleep-stunned and solitary
as anything from Hopper
to a sound-track of rattling iambs:
the track, the train; the track, the train;
the pulse of a city waking.

Bronte After Lunch

Set after set of crests pestle the sea pool wall at the south end.
Today it's a country for young men:

packs of them besting the barbed wire guarding the rock
overhead, daring the drop into mist-glinted turquoise,

or turning and threading the surf to catch-and-pop
into their skill, all will and edge. The sea froths

neutral violence; I'm seething in time, my belly a knot
of the year just rushed by in a blur of contagion

and work. And I can't help but think as I lurk
that this is no longer my nation. Or, if it ever was.

Aubade

The Egyptian builds and he builds
some days he brings friends that help

and I offer them coffee in the height
of Ramadan before entering they leave

their names at the door and I only
ever catch the back of their alphabet

his lips are nearly navy and when
I tell him that I sing he says prove it

I sing badly but I will sing better
the next time that's how the law

of averages works his boss is from Acre
a city that means the sea comes up

to here he tells me they're neighbours
I say I forgot about the border

between Egypt and Israel he laughs
and says no you're not listening

for example if I sang out my window
in the morning he would hear me

Among Treetops

Our apple trees touch at the top
as if having grown up separately
they decided to turn to each other
before it was too late.

I climb to where they meet,
light enough to inch along
their thinnest branches,
not for the apples, but the thrill
of stepping from one tree to another,
testing the strength with my foot,
balancing, airplane arms steady
in the land of wind and branches.

Coming down to earth scares me,
so I call my mother, she climbs halfway,
wraps warm hands around my ankles,
tugging gently, guiding me, *I've got you,*
I've got you, until I'm low enough to leap.
Why go up there, if you're so afraid?
Though she knows. Which of us doesn't?
You never lose the taste for sky walking.

Let me show you, close your eyes,
it is late Autumn, most leaves have fallen,
climb with me, up, up out of the earth,
feel how cold it is here, touch a wet leaf
to your cheek, the sky is only inches away.

Camán/Hurley

The weight of oil in its sword
of wood, a palm of tribal soil
ash-light as summer grass,
as victory, tasting the upside
of history, elixir of legends
on the tongue of heritage,
pride set free from nation,
a silent pterodactyl's swoop,
essence of rain and sweat,
scent of singular purpose:
thwack – sound of perfection.

JANE CLARKE

First Earlies

By rights we'd be standing side by side,
making idle conversation as we wait

to shake hands with our grieving neighbours
after Requiem Mass in Greenan,

but we keep the byroad between us today.
The virus lingers, a low-lying cloud,

until someone asks about planting first earlies.
Advice flies from gateway to gateway:

you can split seed potatoes
as long as each half has a chit,

dig plenty of manure into the drill,
place them a foot apart, a fist deep,

don't forget to earth up the shoots,
they'll be ready for lifting mid-June.

Sharpe's Express, Setanta, Orla,
Slaney, Red Cara, Accord …

our litany's only hushed
by the hearse coming down the road.

empty train

lean your
bike
against the
bridge
stare down
the track

  t
  h
  e
  the
  train
 T H E
T R A I N

wave at
the driver
horn blares
back

another
empty train
exactly
eight o'
clock

Waiting

I wait in silence. Walking for hours through the star clusters of wildflowers, my head enveloped in fog and the feeling you gave me when I last saw you. That I could finally breathe.

I wait fully. Dragging this body along the beach walk, I learn from the stones how to rest. To be still with meaning, as if you were around.

I wait fiercely. For another now, just like those fragile seedlings on the windowsill. I will keep the best inside. Devoid of all things excessive, I fish your words out of every source I meet.

I am the wait. The ruthless heat is at it again. I drink about you at the time-ridden veranda, while suffocating with each mile between us. I swallow my mouthful of dusk and fly where your daydreams dwell.

Shell House Folly, Bushy Park

Every Sunday
she holds us to her ear,
inhales our brittle music
between the snap of fir-tree mulch
and the heron's high scream.

What persists are her sturdy walls,
the deliberate stone on stone
concoction of romance,
and, here and there, a crust of cockle shells
bonded with plaster.

Graffiti glows over fag-ends of a sesh:
broken bottles, cans, a plastic bag.

Every Sunday we remember
our old lives, parties, teenage wilding,
and the waitress in Bewleys
who told us: 'I don't mind if you lie,
as long as you lie beautifully.'

Through the window sockets,
the green eyes of the stagnant lake gleam.

To a Saltmarsh at Midnight

after Rilke

To see it naked – barely discernible from water.
Sky sleeping close to death; dimming down
with each exhale.

Horizon's knife-edge silvered.
How the godwits
stood watch all night like sentries.

Even the moon making its late appearance.
Egret as angel – picking its feathered way
through silt.

To witness it – takes an act of prayer:
to abandon all belief. *Empty yourself,*
it says – *to fill with light.*

Station Man

Well turned out,
has had his breakfast,
you will see him sitting upright
at various tram stops.
Not a commuter, a zigzag man
with a travel pass,
a self-appointed inspector,
mission undisclosed.
He asks for nothing,
but must have the flow.
When not sitting in stations,
a bird talker,
kicker of dogs,
a carpet hedge jumper
who's had his breakfast.

Don't ask about love and friendship.
He wasn't born to this,
but here he is, regardless,
moving when the impulse takes him.
Being there is the thing.
Being anywhere.
Testing civilization.
Not releasing the results.

Na Sráideanna Úd ar Scáileán

Tá na sráideanna ag glaoch –
na búlbhaird bhánaithe, nach mór,
mar a bhíodh aimsir Nollag fadó
am ar fhan chuile dhuine sa bhaile
is a ndearna siopaí gaisce as a n-earraí –
réidh le tús a chur leis na sladmhargaí.

Nár bhreá liom an t-aer úr a análú
éisteacht le ceiliúr na n-éan
gearradh tríd an ollfhairsinge –
madra rua mar chomhluadar agam, seans.

Táim cinnte de rud amháin, áfach:
a luaithe a leagaim boinn mo chos
ar na clocha duirlinge úd
go mbeidh an plód ann romham amach,
seilbh ag múch ar an aer
go mbeidh ceiliúr na n-éan imithe i léig,
an madra rua tar éis filleadh
ar a bhrocais sna bruachbhailte.

San idirlinn tá piorraí ag bachlú sa gharraí
cleimeatas ar foluain ar na ráillí
is glas daingean ar an gcúlgheata.

Those On-screen Streets

The streets are calling –
those near empty boulevards
of Christmas long ago
when everyone stayed home
and shop windows flaunted their wares –
ready for the sales to begin.

How I long to inhale that fresh air
listen to the birdsong
cut through the expanse –
a fox for companion, perhaps.

One thing I am sure of, however:
as soon as my soles touch
those cobblestones
the crowd will be there before me
fumes will have invaded the air
birdsong will have died out
the fox will have returned
to his lair in the suburbs.

Meanwhile pears bud in the garden
clematis wavers on the railings
and the back gate remains locked.

EILÍN DE PAOR

Back at the End of the World

for Barbara

This is how you came to an unnamed spit
of dunes and winter-flooded fields:
the caravan park was too crowded
that summer, your mother couldn't stand it,
so your father drove out, turned off,
picked a field, made an offer.

Clay puddles up in copper pools
where we trudge now through marram trails
carved by long-scrapped dune buggies,
kept up by horses, dogs, the children of the children.

At the sedge-break to the waves, sea pea and holly
catch the pebbled sky, cast back blues to the wheeling terns,
who dive for fish to bring back to their island mates.
We dive our feet into the coarse-grain sand,
choose old songs on our phones –
sing along to the terns, to our mothers.

Wren

The hole in the gable of my house
is home to a wren.
At night, restless in bed, hearing
nothing, I pretend
to nuzzle up to her heartbeat,

the tendrils of her dream a nest
snugged amid encrusted mortar-dust
just beyond my ear.
It's a death, but a sound one,
this sleep ensuing.

Again I rise to life out where
the wren prevails –
now unseen, now tail-up identifiable,
and in the span
of one short morning

centuries seem to pass, as though
the click and trick
of her syllables
were the flitting years, for so
she fuses the song and the listening.

In Judy's Studio

You forget to eat the orange I brought,
but as it shrinks, crinkles,
turns lop-sided, lustreless, you paint it,
and so your forgetfulness

bears other fruit. It's done, I think,
at each visit, but neither you
nor the mould taking cold, clammy hold
will stop, with always more

to do or undo, get through to, the effect
of nothing ever staying just so.
Acceptance or abandonment?
Today, a final touch, a lingering look;

my eyes won't outwear
the greeny white death by which the fruit
has lifted – through daub
and dust of your brushes – onto canvas.

Communion Cake

At seven minutes past midnight, fake tan still to do,
I am making a cake for your Communion:
blood orange and raspberry, swiss meringue buttercream.

No radio to wake small sleepers: just the mixing bowl and me.
I stir in that time I chipped my front tooth drinking wine from
    the bottle
on a hurtling bus;

the morning I markered on shared sheets,
the apple of my anger skin-bursting and monstrous …
you should get a taste of that;

that night I collapsed in a chip shop,
wearing ridiculous purple stilettos. The mother who
tied your laces – see her there, stranger-circled on the dirty floor;

divorced joys of morning cigarettes, kissing boys on other planets,
heart sky-sized and full, body music-wrapped – in they go,
alongside that jump from a ten-foot wall in heels and a ballgown.

Finally, the morning I rang in sick, first day in a new job, to stay
in bed with your young father. In it leaps, just before the final
    stir-up.
This thick batter of blunders and misreckonings, I spoon into tins.

The oven hums readiness for transformation, separateness debunked
in its warm belly. Beloved, it's scary, but a liberation, too,
when we discover the woman in front walked mapless,
                              through a trail of spilt milk.

Granddaughter

You offer your upturned hand
to the wonder of water falling.
Drops gather in the small cup
of your palm; I name it for you
     – rain –
and you give it back to me,
the tired world, all new again.

Curragh of Kildare

My childhood playground,
open sky landscape, sweeping
east to west. Secret scrub corridors
for hunters of chance, for pinching

sap from nature's crown.
The military graveyard – hip hillock fixed,
we climb the camel's back
to rest beneath a thinly drawn elm.

Heroes of WWI, quilt-turf covered.
Cracked tombstones sigh:
We are but ships on a freezing wave,
sinking now. Child cloud-blown

downhill, coming to rest in Donnelly's Hollow
between pools of shadow-cold. Motherless dark,
creeping giants of fortune, my Curragh reflects
your wide wind-sweep, your relentless swallow.

River, at Dusk

On the far bank, Mad Sullivan's sucklers turn away from me
    and go still.
They are watching a figure cross the field; something ill-defined,
a ghost or a hunted priest, the *Marcach* maybe. How they part
    and show
him to water like a man damned. Bellies hardened with rushes
    and gorse,
they snip again a dole of summer grass, or what's shown of it –
their legs plunging frightened cuts in the soil, Rural Electrification
    polls
bothering elk bones, Holocenic shells, and hidden men.
A Polly calf thrashes flies from her head, the blur of yellow tags
making her a flower-crowned Alpine milker; a leveret in the corner
of the field does not see me, and the figure stops to watch the
    moon go up.
The grass is growing over my feet now. Hatches of fly parade like
    tall ships,
trout slash at them under the Sally trees; an otter pulls himself up
    the bank;
somewhere, a buzzard mews, and a bullock shoulders a gate in the
    last light.
I look up to see a swallow drop from the clouds as though he were
    struck,
or had finally, after weeks of flight, caught the first tentative
    glimpse of home.

Passerine, Born

The brood mare is staring at something in the corner of her stable.
In my hand, a swallow's nest goes crumbling: shingle of clay and
    calf hair,
beak marks inside-out like a gutted house – all sunlit wallpapers,
linen closets agape. Up the yard, the sheepdog is pacing and circling
the chain-links of his pen. I close my eyes and murmur a hymn
we learned as children, guess the Latin words, pick them like insects
from air. She is marble now, the mare, little Naomhóg smoothed
with wind and the warmth of desperate hands. Swallows come to line
the stable wall – a summer funeral, beaks full with fat rattles of news,
rubbing and clinking, scratching like plates – they wait for the
    whites of her eyes;
for ears to slip like the bolt of a rifle. I see then that I have wings,
the cat having left them for me in dust and droplets by the stable door.
And when I close my eyes, they break my back like legs of a
    stitch-trapped foal.
Quick and wet we fly, the wings and I, make some wounded bark
    our home;
all night I pull these feathers from my back, but when I wake,
    I am set in stone.

The Rough Guide to Climbing Carrauntoohil

They say when the journey is long, arrival is sweet.
On Carrauntoohil's slopes we scale twilight's brink
while sundogs claw false dawns, snapping at fear,
slaying inertia to the beat of voices, the rhythm
of words that recall what we lost on the way,
the field of debris illuminating how we go on.
The sun shines on half the world but the stars
see us all: our brief, exiled rituals of grief,
the determined placing of each foot forward,
embossed on the precious scripts of our legacy.
Our courage-songs grow as the shadows fade,
then ring out at the summit. We stand tall, laugh,
cry, gather round; reach for each other, embrace
and leave slowly, tying prayer-rags on outcrops;
each one a single, sustaining note in our collective
poem-song, flying in the wind, fluttering after us.

Cliff Road

Flat deep water,
colour of tin
elderflower grass sea air
tin clouds breasting cliffs
girls jumping into tin water
buoyed up like corks.
At the first rumble
of thunder, I stare skywards
as if I might catch
you staring back.

Whistle Across Time

Over Loch Laíg waves
yellow-billed song of blackbird
cast from whin blossoms

With cancer and pandemic comes urgency to find
where on our shore a forgotten monk
wrote this 9th century verse.

I haven't heard a blackbird whistle over Loch Laíg,
but today, a robin peeks out among whin blossoms,
lands near my feet and begins to sing.

Again and again he flies from bush to strand.
Flutter of belief – he's greeting me, showing me
it was here.

> *The italicized haiku is 'Blackbird of Belfast Lough', a 9th century poem*
> *translated by Tim Dwyer. Loch Laíg – Old Irish name for Belfast*
> *Lough, meaning 'inlet of the calf'.*

In Case

a letter to my friend

Late morning light, tiny prisms flicker
among the pebbles at low tide.

I scan my body for symptoms and signs:
a scratch in the throat, a sudden chill,

a new, unusual pain.
I wish you could see this black-backed gull
landing in the estuary, towering among the flock,

his breast the most brilliant white I have seen
since my childhood dream of the moment
before I was born.

City Sparrow

Sparrow likes hanging around handbags and shoes
Waiting for the flecks of cured meats and truffle infused
Breads to fall from the fingers of those above.
Sparrow was born under the restaurant eves

Where cake crumbs snowed down on her daily.

Sparrow waits for days for the magpie man with his
White string tails to unnest the tables and set the places
For the people to come and drop the crumbs from the linen sails.
When no one appears, Sparrow's hunger drives her away.

She must dig deep to access some country birding ways.

Sparrow learns to quit her flitting among the feet and listen to the
Aphids and other hairy moving things give their location away.
She sticks her beak in the dirt and eats the clay-crusted flesh whole.
While dreaming of showers of seed-crusted crackers

Sparrow wonders why she has never tried this kind of birding before.

Garden Shed

Through the shed's squat door,
I am back to a tower block
in East Berlin before the fall

where every night at ten
the State-employed caretaker,
with the B-movie limp,

locked our flat door from the outside
and where, at midnight,
the man in the flat above

dropped empty beer bottles
onto the concrete plaza below,
glass exploding as he roared

expressions in old German
(consisting, we learned later, of a series
of agricultural curses

directed largely at his mother).
Our door unlocked again at dawn
although by whom, we never saw.

Walking with Mary Oliver

I'm at peace, with you
   I forget chasing sales
     or yesterday. I turn off
the TV, put down

my smartphone.
   With you I want to
     walk slowly
to the mountains,

collect blackberries,
    smell flowers,
      fall in love
with a hummingbird,

watch the landscapes
  change season. Study
    trees and breath,
the moss, a swan, an otter.

Because I'm alive,
   to sing my heart's
    song, even
as the rains return.

The Year of Water

first I thought it was the sound of a drill
but through a hole in the ceiling
water thundered onto the kitchen floor

my mother-in-law's house   & in my own mother's house
an overflow tank flooded the bathroom floors
got that sorted with a telescope ladder to the attic

third   the percolation system in our garden
      the air vents filling with water
sorted that with a new drain to the left far corner

then there's the river-flow in Raymond Carver's poems
more broad-shouldered than holding back on what one means to say
& there's another poet's *Nobody*   at sea   with no resting place

last there's a poetry editor who favours profusion
living with someone who favours precision
one can't help wondering what their love-making is like

Menhir

Take the R697 North from
Carrick-on-Suir, after 6 kms
turn left for Faugheen,
in 300 metres look left and
you will see the standing stone.

I cannot say who
put the stone here.

I cannot explain how
the stone got here.

I cannot say why
the stone stands here.

What does it commemorate?

I can say that it is Silurian
slate and like the bole of
an oak, I encircle it.

I rest by it.

I can say that a fourteenth
century quarry is nearby,
that quarrying has ceased –

and Oliver, the farmer,
says it stands here for cows
to rub their backs against.

staves

||||

A door into the bank of the Camac
is the tally of a river rune people
sweet sulphur of thorn

⊥

'There are all these little insects!'
a corona of midges
'Good. We have Friends.'

⊷

I tried to blow a dandelion
clock, forgot
I was wearing a mask

т

I don't think I'm much cop
at this observational stuff

I could take a piss
against a silver birch and reflect
that the shrinking *vishnukranta*
shat on by Arun Kolatkar
might be glossed *morning glory*

⊞

Twigs laid out beside a flowerbed
in the War Memorial Gardens:
ogham hazel

Lutyens designed
those squat magazines
as reading rooms

ᚈ

An aulfella beards
me by Kilmainham Gaol
he hasn't seen another man
in *one of these* all day
his own, bunched beneath his chin

ᚌ

more power to you/yours

rest

The Comfort of Mallards

In the dark unseen they hold a private
conversation, their voices rising off
the river mist-like, melody of moss
and ink, broken on occasion by the soft
splash of a newcomer to the congress.
Wisdom in their mournful affirmations,
old and soothing as mud; truths pass between
their nodding beaks, slipping moonlit over
glassy ripples, clinging to riverbank
reeds, the shimmering backs of water rats,
like pearls translating into air, into
breath, expanding the lungs of trees, filling
the branching trees of my lungs, it's there, they
say, what you came looking for, there. There, there.

After

After the hospital everything was new again
on the drive home, like that time I came back from China.
Cows in fields. Summer hedges, cow parsley, overgrown verges.
Once in the door, even my tatty curtains, cardboard boxes
in the living room, dusty windows, were rinsed clean.
And the colours. Pink! Yellow! Green!

The dog looked at me. *You. It's you.*
At night I wanted to climb out
of my skin. The bed, too much a bed.
All I craved was the hard, inhospitable floor
– *What are you doing down there, mum?* –
until cold numbed me into a blessèd doze.

One night I lay awake for hours,
stared at the same spot above the wardrobe
where the disused TV cable hangs down.
Only months later I realise there is no wardrobe there.
Just the blank wall and the flex.

There was more. So much more.
But after everything, all I want to do is stand
in the corner shop to look at fruit and veg
stacked in their neat rows, choose my own milk
from the fridge, even gaze at bottles of bleach,
4-packs of toilet roll
and marvel. This, all this.

Minke Whale

A break in the line, the comma
of a dorsal slices the corner
of the eye like a new planet
seen from the windows of a cell.
The act of writing is a common
migration between the seasons,
continues apace, even doubles down,
every word its own significant sound.
A trawler tracks, trails moving pools
of darkness, pollock a greenish
black splash in the ocean.
Minutes pass, white belly shifts, rises
up beyond the Sovereigns unbound,
an old presence seeking new ground.

Vision, North Antrim

The Carrickmore Road hems my parish of Culfeightrin
where its townlands – Broughanlea, Drumaroan, Tornabodagh,
    Tornaroan –
dip their skirts into the Sea of Moyle
(with a last flounce of grassy clefts, precarious caravans
and a beading of white houses)
before relinquishing themselves
to waves that take the colour of the sky, a jumbled grey.

Here all is profusely, wetly, Irishly grey or green;
even the light arrives through a dampened veil yet
pagoda roofs, crimson
– the hedges are full of them.
Each dangles a furl of imperial purple,
a firework spurting tiny comets
down to a mossy sky.

That veil's dissolving. I see
sulphur-yellow sunbursts in the ditch;
hard globes of military red strung on the bushes
for a brash tattoo; cockades – vermilion –
tossed up among the brambles by a hidden crowd;
medals of cerise pinned to the ferny cliffs; corsages of
hot mauve, burnt orange, the colour *lucifer* ...

Is it because I've reached this edge
that I have eyes at last to see
what has been burning always
within my coolest day?

After these months of paring-down, let me keep
my vision stripped,
here, where there is no further north.

Locale

Mountains live in deep time,
their weathered rock fast
asleep in the night.

Things come alive when
they're not yours to keep –
like the surge of damsons

in hedgerows or a turtle
dove's silence before
winter in Africa.

Orientation, consolation –
don't take for granted
the cypress tree's look

of an Egyptian obelisk,
how it anchors the sky.
Landscape is a verb

to conjugate nearby.
Heeling a sapling in
is like planting a word

dropped from the dictionary.
Acorn, bluebell, catkin –
they read me like a book.

Foxes

The world stills like this creature
at the end of the path

with flattened skull, upright ears
and bushy tail sweeping over sand.

The sea twitches. A blade of fear
pricks in the time it takes

to look away, its lore close enough
to touch. Its eyes don't drop

but hold my stare in the house
of the stare, with its wall of wind

and looping sky. A light of sorrow
burns in its eyes as if minding

the time cubs surrounded her
at the bottom of a den.

We gauge each other politely
from a distance, panting softly.

There's always a thrill that needs
no danger to make it real.

Sirens

for Duncan

At intervals, in our edgy little town,
that shrill note rises and falls

and our collie answers it. He stands
in the back yard, lifts his wolfy muzzle

and adds something desolate and beautiful –
a lament, a full-throated dirge –

to the great book of warnings and wounds:
sheep torn from the flock,

a human slipped from the pack.
Only a dog knows how to sing

to a siren. Here he comes,
a blue halo flashing on his head,

keen as the wind floating over the roofs,
herding the traffic aside.

The End, Etc.

The world ended on October 22, 1844,
as William Miller had predicted it would.

We are living in its aftermath, along with
all the other Millerites who suffered through
what became known as The Great Disappointment,

to regroup as The Adventists, then
The Seventh Day Adventists who now
have a worldwide membership of 20 million souls.

The human mind is a stepped-on ant
that miraculously unsquishes itself, to invent
Braille, write *A Brief History of Time*

or develop a new strain, something that will prove
impervious to the slightest trickle of doubt
or the weight of a toddler's sandal, which is

the weight of the world insufferably carrying on.

The Robin

At this stage it seems clear
the robin is hitting on my mother,
first sizing her up as she reads in the back garden,
soaking up those July heatwave rays.
He hops from brick to brick,
ready to be rebuffed at any moment,
and day by day gets closer,
eventually daring to take the seat next to her
(you're in there now, lad).
His red is duller than you'd expect,
or maybe real life is not a glossy Christmas card,
and my mother tells me birds moult in the summer –
learned in primary school and forgotten,
because what use is it knowing these things,
in our busy office lives?

Apart

The advisory booklet says,
because my rubbish lungs
and the compromising position
in which my immune system finds itself
put me among those most likely to expire,
my wife and I must, for the duration,
remain at least one metre apart
and I shouldn't wander
beyond the front garden
except for my weekly safari
to put out the bins.

If she has an itch,
it's okay for me to scratch
her back with the sweeping brush
without the written permission
of a Garda Sergeant.

But if she kills me
for talking too much, as she likely will,
the Minister for Justice
has signed an order requiring her
to do so with a twenty-eight-inch shotgun
(with which she will be provided)
or at the very least a regulation length
Samurai sword. It won't be pretty.
But neither, the booklet assures me, am I.

Meantime, there are other possibilities:
couples such as us
are still legally permitted

to do things to each other
with a Marks & Spencer cotton dishcloth attached
to what looks like a mop handle;
or by making imaginative use
of a retractable ostrich feather duster.

I worry it could lead
in the long run to her coming
at my most vulnerable bits
with the hedge clippers;
and where would I be then?
Though the cat assures me:
I'm there already.

some day

there will be time
to Hoover
behind the sofa
to separate
Mega Bloks from Lego
to wipe down window sills
varnish
garden furniture we let sit
all winter
not knowing to lock it away
some day
laundry will not need respun
the microwave
won't be crusted in bean juice
some day I will paint
my nails
no smudges
I will take you to Newcastle
I'll catch
your watchful eyes
on someone else
You'll tell me
what mattered
some day

The Skylark and I

The skylark and I have traded places,
I reel and churr all day and she's great
with paperwork, a natural shredder.
It was difficult at first to master
a voice that pulses so close
to the heart, where each lung draws
its song independent from the other,
holding air and refrain in the same
breath, but oh sweet syrinx, the sound!

Each dusk, we meet, her with a glass
of Merlot, me diving for gnats,
she talks office hours, utility bills, tax,
how thin her skin has become, how
her hair has lost its curl. I jump
into her palm, peck its lines. She smiles.
At night, while I watch out for crow
or stoat or owl, I hear her sometimes
trying to sing, listen to how the breath
catches in her throat, listen to how
she invests so much in holding
together that one single note.

The Etymology of this Day in Spring

Dawn. Black grouse lekking, undertails fanned like lyres.
Lek – Norse for child's play, like the lambs flutter-jumping
the fields in their tight new skins, umbilical cords thin
and dripping. The knackerman is collecting the dead

from each farm gate along the dale, mothers mostly,
hock, pestern, fetlock hard set skyward. The moor is dry
but giving underfoot and the sphagnum moss suffers for it.
Skylarks drift into fescue, the gate by the marsh moans
its rosary of scales. *Festina Lente* it seems to say
while the world shoots arrows over its shoulder. Brother,
your death floats around like all the other scents the spring
wind whips up – lanolin and daffodil, nettles claiming
the roads in the absence of traffic. The rooks clamour
at this lack of roadkill ambushing rabbits as they bolt
from their burrows. Hah! How quickly a power-vacuum
whirlwinds through our carrion parliaments. Poachers
were here last night. I turned on the light, *a pox
be upon them* I said and didn't regret saying it, fingers
gripping cricket bat. Footpads, mosstroopers, reevers,
no strangers to this dark low house and its wind-split
rowan where the noose was once secured and tightened
but whose branches are now a posse of buds and light,
fluorescent as the surveyors in high-vis jackets, who like
the easterly fret, have suddenly appeared at the *lek*
(Cumbrian word for lake, Wordsworth used it) wielding
dumpy levels like cudgels, something about too much silt
in the clay sheath and the concrete gauze not holding water.
But we have always known in our hearts (haven't we?)
all dams break, no chamber can bear such weight, not even
the clouds in all the lenticular grandeur of a sun-spilt hour.
Does each droplet yearn to go back to the ocean or wish
to stay above it? The enter key on the laptop has stopped
working so I am unable to return. It is these small things,
not the apocalyptic, that defeat us in the end, when we can
no longer default to factory settings or be what we have
always been – *facere* – maker, doer, agent. Dusk. The only
agent at this hour is the moon, the closest it will ever be
this year, fleshy and rising in its playground of stars,
indifferent to the pull it exerts or the distant between us.

Finding our feet

Early on we worried
how we would learn the steps

in this barn the size of us
standing in a square

facing ourselves listening
for the caller's patter

praying our feet and hearts
would find the same rhythm

as strangers who were neighbours
and now were partners.

He tapped the mic and sang:
Roll away to a half sashay

and we held hands to *Box
the gnat and wrong way grand*

keeping our shape
with a nervous laugh

sorry for stepping on toes
in this barn the size of us

not sure how we got here
but sure we had to dance

circle left and *do-si-do*
it wasn't yet time for home.

On the very last note of the cadence,

the sky tumbled. It crumpled,
in the breaths of a noon turning to night.
Clouds spread on the streets like salts.

The paths of Temple Bar that are paved
like burnt buns on blackened factory trays,
whited, like paper.

It was the formal call to mulled wine.
Throws with scents of loved ones.
Laughter in burning houses.

A darkness, affable, and vain.

Surfers at Doonloughan

This must be the longest lockdown yet,
deepening troughs and sharper gales
are swelling the Atlantic while I wait
in the lee of a dune, and stay down.
The shower passes but the clouds remain,
we are stormbound wintering this out.
But meanwhile, surf is up, breaking broad
and clean; surfers in their water gear
have come, now they are poised, they're set.
Gulls tack and veer as the blue surge
breathes, then one surfer goes, gets clear
on a wave that's high but casually furls.
He threads its crest, staying on board
a one-man show flung perfectly to shore.

Immersion

April, a new way of the sun falling,
The wilful accents of the people,
The colours of the flag
On the clothes they wore.

A young man's coy credentials,
The first days of immersion
In parks and fountains;
Life in small rooms,
Before leaving in a burnt September.

Forever after, grasping at gauzy webs
And tendrils hanging from airy trees.

Walking The Dog

Rosco pays the poet's full attention –
alert to every track and trace,
and all those tiny airborne sounds
that constitute the perfect silences –
birdsong, airplanes, mowers;
that tinny, rhythmic hammering
from half a mile away.

He misses nothing.
And if and when I drift, he stops
to bring me back; his stubborn tug
like a pike at the Pump House Shore
just as rod and line and trailing bait –
even the creaking boat itself –
have been, in reverie, forgotten.

I love our danders round the block.
A dreamtime circuit, a pavement loop
where all is memory and wonder.
Yesterday, this warm, black, biodegradable bag
of what my mother called dog's dirt
had me thinking – *Jack steps home
from market with his bag of magic beans.*

This morning it's a heavy, leather purse
tossed by a dandy to an urchin in the street;
when I hep it in my hand it rings aloud
with gleaming sovereigns. Rosco sits
and tilts his head, and together we ponder
what is possible – what is magical –
in this unexpected fortune of jingle and tap.

fremdkörper

when the magpies stop singing
& your lips fall asleep
because you were taught silence
&the place goes deaf
because someone ejected you –
fremdkörper

the dimples between your mouth
&chin would stop
your patter would stop
your claps would stop the lilacs
would stop, cindy would stop the cars
would stop the olur would
stop the world would stop the
pasta would stop the owls would stop the birch
would stop when the wind would stop the 'gâr would stop
the brötchen would stop
paradise at my knees would stop your curls
would stop the
crinkle by your honey eyes
would stop

I would lay it all beneath your feet –
the cliffs at howth
sultanahmet's minarets
steppes of those gone –
I would lay pyramids of baklava
and mounds of ice cream
on a warm may day
at odeonsplatz by the

royal adelaide &
bürgerpark pankow by
the grand canal&
the microcosm
in my blood
& tell you –

tread fiercely
like you own
the place.

How to Mend a Sole with Pliers

Esilding ar zhaghında kördim seni,
Sırghandı qayıq qılıp ötkiz meni …

I saw you at the other side of the Esil (river),
Make a boat from your earring and allow me passage …
 – Birzhan Sal (Kazakh poet, 19th c.)

Strong coffee grounds ache between your gums
your hands a hot stove on which to cook up creations
with boats for tools & a land on a wooden map,
your hands hem tennis dresses from last season &
make a way of speaking, your mother hands
a sanctuary, I am always asking
to borrow the pliers – in truth I seek your qol,
garlic-smelling, raw meat-smelling qol,
like each half-year, when they haul the whole
animal into our hallway & you chip away
at it, hot flesh still beating, still steaming,
slice each section according to tradition –
jambas, asıq jilik, jaurın –

we hold heart & liver & kidney
like medical students & estimate the weight
of a soul. We bag each fragment, eat
quırdaq with fried onions as the glow
of lights turn against the planet's back.

The landbridge to your hands is closed,
I seek you from ether lines –

CLAIRE-LISE KIEFFER

Apis mellifera mellifera

The dark Irish honey bee, a subspecies
of the European honey bee, has adapted
to thrive in all that the filthy Irish weather
has to throw at it, I read. Here, where each
man and woman carries a heavy death,
dealing with grief is a honey bee, darting from
flower to flower like a dance on hot coals,
don't stand still for fear of burnt soles –
a dance many-times learned and passed down,
and when I clumsily traipse, lightly clad
in my one funeral – what a sheltered life I lead –
around a corner, there is another hanging corpse
or worse, a brother, when I least expect it. O nation
of beekeepers, when I think I can embrace
one of your citizens, they are already far away,
dancing, dancing, bright and merry ghost lights
over a dark draught.

Planting

This garden is the centre of a wheel,
the sun revolves around it like clockwork.
I use a spade to breach the crust, a fork
to break up clods. I pick out stones and feel
the sun's heat on my back. My knee joints creak.
I've learned the difference between work and rest,
regret the years spent idling at a desk.
The blisters on my hand mark me as weak.
Repetition. Dig and turn clay over,
mop brow, savour these authentic actions.
The fearless robin eyes the wriggling worm –
she is so close. Give in to the lover
who is here, all others are distractions;
plant the seed, water and make firm.

After the party

Oisín's lost his phone, and Oisín's dog
is running wild through the bluing garden,
the kind of theatrical spirit that leads you

to that boundary place
where people feel inevitably met.
I've walked beyond the open gate

towards the last traces of sun,
a swatch of salmon in a deepening wash,
to the edges of where other people live,

where, finding nothing lost, I turn

and walk back up the lane;
she is there,
walking towards me out of the inevitable twilight.

Now leaf shadows wing the scene;
we move to face the sound of animals
in the field where Oisín walks with an empty lead.

I put my arm around her waist
and know I'm going to miss her terribly
when Oisín's dog emerges from the trees.

Tower Bay, Portrane

Everything gathers light;

sea-spray splicing air, slick
of eel-grass over green-laced rock,

spindrift breezing, and in the distance,
the sun rolls down Lambay's shiver

of strand, rituals of ocean, their rhythms
and spills, the kayak's foam-cuffed

trail now a vein of vanishing
ripples. Wave-pleats fold

and crease, while out
along the horizon, the pause

of settled light, brightness honed
to a scalpel

and the whole world curves
to meet the cleave

of a sea-gull's wing.

On The Road to Loughatorick

Locked in a world of pills and syringes,
the door closed to familiar faces,
the behind-the-counter transformed,
fronted by a screen to the outside world,
the cologne of Yardley or Lancôme
overthrown by the sanitised scent
of methylated spirits and absolute alcohol.

The busy dispensary of banter and chat
is reduced to labels and printers, phones
and panic. The rows of luscious lipsticks
abandoned, lips disappear behind masks.
The urgency of the day rings in my ears
into the night, revisiting and revision
of guidelines and protocols
roiling in turmoiled dream.

Then driving out to Bridie's house
in the early May evening light,
from over Lough Derg a lone heron
takes itself into the air
with barely a flap … and I wonder
was it for Bridie's prescription alone
that I found myself
on the road to Loughatorick.

Between Tonduff and Maulin

Weighty clouds glower and somersault
across a high plain of moss and heather
like an Old Testament storm in a Children's Bible.
The sun squints through rain, mocks revelation.

When curtains of mist fray and disperse,
aqua-blue peaks of west Wicklow beckon.
Not that the wind chill isn't bitter.
Underfoot, black peat turns treacherous

as butter. Bog pools hide in wait
beneath the whispering moor
like bear traps in a forest.
Often the path wears clean to granite

glinting with mica. In my veins like lightning –
our existence precarious, an inkling.

Frederick May in Clontarf

Another afternoon inside the blue
embrace of the rain shelter on the prom.
Still too early to go back to his room
with the nuns. His ears are acting up:
the transistor hearing-aid makes the noise
in his head no less infernal. Sometimes
he thinks it would have been more bearable
without music. The sea only the sea
and nothing in it but fish and pink-
tinted shells. If spaces that held music
were suddenly empty, available,
what sluice might open? Would love pour in
like a flight of swallows, survivors to praise
with all the silent music of his heart?

Our Statues Go Unwatched

Outside Trinity, Edmund Burke
removes his pocket handkerchief
to rub the pigeon droppings from his brow.
Oliver Goldsmith puts down the book
he has been reading since 1864.
Molly Malone immune to fever, drops her barrow
and enjoys a stroll, no eyes on her breasts.
Daniel O'Connell descends from his granite plinth
to inspect the bullet holes in Courage's chest.
Connolly meets Larkin at Liberty Hall to discuss
the next stage in the collective struggle.
Joyce retraces Leopold's steps
but Barney Kiernan's and Davy Byrne's are closed.
The two Luke Kellys unleash a guttural punch
The Auld Triangle in unison across the dirty river.
The hair stands on the Talking Ladies necks;
they soon return to putting this crumbling world in order.
Countess Markievicz strides with purpose towards
the waking famine sculptures on the North Dock.
Oscar Wilde has seen death in Man's eyes
and decides it is preferable to remain reclined.

Fragments from a Local Odyssey

Dark hoodie
  hangs
        from a manicured hedge.

Poplar fluff
  blankets
        the grass and path.

Heineken bottles
  unopened
        at the end-house wall.

Young bullfinch
  flutters
        water over its wings.

Fold-up chair
  submerged
        in the lake.

Magpies and squirrels
  rage
        territorial war.

Telephone book
  blackens
        at the 27 bus stop.

Trumpet flowers
  survive
        in the cavity of a fence.

Sunbeam
  illuminates
        the charred remains of foil.

Baby Scan June 2020

for Hannah Kate

In this picture you are swirling galaxies –
The Milky Way, Andromeda, dark matter
and ether gathering. We read you like

a sea chart without a compass.
You are drift, unplumbed depth, we see
shooting stars for centuries of women

whose forgotten lives gather in your skin.
You are all drumlin, cliff, sea and gannet dive,
we trace your shape, make sense of hieroglyph.

Your arm is raised, are you hiding from this time
or weightless in a deep pool, dreaming in sound,
the rise and fall of breath, the sea cave pulse of heart.

A Visit to the Nursing Home

Early Summer 2020

Our talk is an old lane just wide enough for two,
where clay ditch and stone wall catch fern,
wild raspberry and, in shade, a violet.

No one knows who was first to walk this lane,
it makes a track from one wild space to another
across a bog land, uncharted, wide as sky.

My mother's route of talk travels
down years of greetings, words of comfort,
love, pitch and rhyme.

Her stories stretch like high branches, make
a fragile splintered roof where we shelter.
Today she is off to bring in the cows, or to Bundoran,

but sometimes our feet step in tune along this path,
then the earth smells of summer.

JAKI McCARRICK

Sweeney as a girl

Up here with the crags and windbush
I look down on the amber world
and I say truthfully to you,
I do not miss it.

I hate its vacuous Facebook self.
I hate its plagues and smoke and mirrors.
For I have come to love
what my grandparents had
and my parents abandoned:
the quiet, wild earth.

For the brief time I am here
I have the real earth,
without double-glazing,
the freedom of the broad valleys
without Capitalism.

The grey in my hair
is pure white wire,
my smile a row of crags.

All over Oriel
I seek out the sparse woods
and miss nothing of it all
down there in the town,
only my dark hair,
a lover's hand to stroke it.

> In the medieval Irish work 'Buile Suibhne', Sweeney is a king
> exiled to the wilds of the north-east of Ireland.

DEIRDRE McMAHON

Grooming

May 2020

The black crow
perched on the pony's back
plucks dun tufts of winter coat,
smoothing its way to summer.

This Summer

This summer our house, an aviary,
Bulged with bird after bustling bird.
Nightly, an owl's cry passed down the valley
Until it almost could not be heard.

Remembering Mannin Bay

for Ena Lavelle & Dermot Dunnion,
Coral Strand, Mannin Bay, Ballyconneelly, Connemara,
53.4402 –10.0629

Fighter jets have cut the Belfast sky like shrapnel,
the down-blast a menace
of sound. Perhaps death itself
remembered I exist
and, like an after-thought,
arrived, heat-seeking
and suddenly to find me,
then teasing, veered off.

Here I am; my desk is dry –
a proxy beach for the cold-water corals
I put into my pocket as keepsakes
the last time I saw the ocean.

This city is holding its breath,
the moon a searchlight watching us;
nothing at ground level moves without scrutiny,
and anything could happen, or so it seems.

And so, when the scouts among the swifts
arrive overhead today, I am poring over
the shorthand bycatch of Hy-Brasil –
pink maërl, a garden of lace
white as alabaster, blue and pearly
mussel shells, molluscs of ochre, bronze, lavender –
cockles and glass burnished by sand,
a shallow tide, the weather.

Hold on, they say. *Hunker down*, they say.
Ocean. Ocean. Ocean. Mannin Bay.

*Belfast. 8th May 2020 – the 75th anniversary of VE Day,
Remembering 14th March 2020, the last day we were out
before going into lockdown.*

Unapproved Gravedigging

> *Cork County Local Authorities accept no responsibility for injuries*
> *sustained in the course of unapproved gravedigging, including*
> *voluntary gravedigging.*
> – Sign at St Mary's Churchyard, Schull, County Cork

Digging your own grave is just selfish. Unsolicited digging
of someone's else grave is intrusive and potentially demoralising.
It may result in injury to the unapproved gravedigger
or to the old person withholding approval. Involuntary gravedigging
is a neglected but concerning aspect of the problem.
Involuntary gravedigging takes three forms.
First is coerced gravedigging, which rarely ends well.
It generally occurs in situations involving a breach of other
Cork County Local Authorities Regulations and Guidelines.
Tourists should take care to avoid being drawn into this kind
   of scenario.
Next, there is compulsive gravedigging, an anti-social addiction
to which even middle-aged, middle-class visitors may succumb.
Don't get carried away. When the fun stops, put down the shovel.
Finally, there is involuntary gravedigging *stricto sensu*,
generally occurring during sleep or a seizure. It is best addressed
by gently waking the unapproved gravedigger or treating him or her
with anti-convulsant medication. To learn more about these issues,
visit www.corkcountylocalauthorities.ie/stopdigging.
Enjoy West Cork's churchyards and cemeteries with moderation.

Sun Bath

The linguist who washed up beside me on the beach
Tells me *sunne* in Old English was feminine
Something I'd intuited long ago in class:
I tested Mother Sun, Sister Sun on my tongue
And saw her ride a white horse across the heavens,
Her corona a wreath of sunflowers round her head.

And brought home, lying there, that everything in reach,
The linguist, the gull, the sandfly, oestrogen,
Adrenaline, melanin, breath itself that passed
Through my aging body was her immortal song.
I drowsed in the fret of my petty obsessions
Tracking a mote on the inside of my eyelid,

A fleck of colour – intense cerulean blue,
Surrounded by a nimbus of emerald green
Like a planet wandering against the fixed stars.
If there is any consolation to be found
In the place I go where light can barely reach me
Where I hold on by my fingertips to this life

It is our absolute dependence on our true
Mother: how she offers a sense of proportion;
How in the future, in five or so billion years
Her work will be done with this earth, the very ground
Of our being, of memory, of prophesy.
Mercury, Venus, our own blue planet engulfed,

Consumed in our glorious Mother's death throes –
A redemptive perspective as that ant mooches
Across my sketchbook, across my light-addled lines.

The Liberties, April 2020

These budding branches right above,
This dazzling sunshine;
A guilty walk around my redbrick block –
I tread no further. A month or more
my neighbours wouldn't bother
with gauze curtains or blackout blinds.

The rowan crown's gossipy with songbirds.
The nosy parkers pry inside and tweet
Among themselves the feather-raising news:
The humans are entrapped, encaged, endangered;
Where lovers used to toss us crumbs,
The foxes play a ruse.

Do songbirds spot in one of those windows
A boy's foot slowly swaying side to side?
(His puffy toe just wriggled off a fly).
He slouches on a couch with his phone.
A slanted shadow rests upon his face.
Sunbathing feet, why should he even know
The stranger sees him from the lonesome street.

Half Moon Swim Club

Southwall Swim under the Super Flower Moon, May 2021

We are looking
in the wrong direction.
Dozens of us
in iridescent swim caps
bobbing over Dublin Bay
bathing ourselves in the bare night.
We are looking up at the clouds
the sky, the heavens
as if we have forgotten
how to look ahead
so used to the cold
the pale sting of our skin
against the bald darkness
water lapping at our chins
until, all at once
we see it

the moon
blooming in front of us
a chrysanthemum of flame
its warm arch rising from the sea
colossal and awake, climbing
the sky, electrified
in full-blooded light, a keyhole
to a different world
pulling us closer, pulling
us forward, out of our
year-long sleep.

There is a madness, a lunacy
in wanting to be alive
to dive headfirst into the dark
inhale the salt, the tide
the burning air of twilight
to watch the moon lift
over a hushed city
its reflection spreading before us
like an open road

Lockdown:

      from *lock*, an old Germanic word
meaning *to fasten,* a fastening mechanism, a turn
of phrase changing according to the preposition
to determine people or things, as in, *to lock in*
pertaining to people, or *to lock up,* pertaining
to things or the chamber itself, i.e. to lock up the house
or to lock up valuables, in North American usage
to lock up refers to prisoners, i.e. my mother was
locked up, meaning my mother was a thing, which is
not surprising, she stopped being real a long time ago,
but now that she is dead, it is a problem of direction,
whether to look up or down when speaking, and from this
comes the second part of a compound word, *down:*
an adverb meaning descent, or a noun, meaning
a bundle of feathers to keep us warm as arctic birds,
and when taken together, *lockdown,* a term first used
in the 1970s when referring to inmates in prisons or
patients in psychiatric hospitals during riots,
was a method to keep them safe from themselves,
snug as small caged birds strip searched, chanting
Attica, Attica, into the hollow, point-blank dark,

and later in the '90s, the term came to refer to schools
and children, meaning a boy walks down the hall
with a Glock 19, Mossberg 500, or a Smith & Wesson
his parents gave him for Christmas, and you have
fifteen seconds or less to barricade the door, jump away
from the window, call your mother, hide under a desk,
hello, can you hear me? and hope for the best
like a snail on barbed wire

and now in 2020, we watch the clouds multiply
as if the sky was contagious, and we, too,
learn not to move, like a child stuffed in a closet
waiting for the footsteps to fade, meaning
it is no longer safe to touch the living, no longer safe
to say goodbye to our dead, we peer at them
through dirty windows instead, mouthing the words,
hello, can you hear me? as they take their last
breath: meaning, grief is a lost key to a house we are
not allowed to enter, like a doorway during the bubonic
plague: *Lord have mercy* written over a cross in red paint
where the lymph nodes of the sick swelled like black balloons,
and centuries later, the Victorians called it Black Death
with their penchant for the perfect little obsidian dress,
and nearly 200 years afterward, a new millennium of purples
and pinks, a virus, heavy as a disco ball, bright as badly dyed
Easter eggs cracking across every hemisphere
until even the pope grows afraid, the frayed sound
of a helicopter drifting from one hospital to the next,
like incense trembling through an empty basilica,
while angels hover in white plastic gowns
their faces shielded and blurred
placing body after body into the earth,
like small pale bulbs knitted through the dirt,
glowing like starlight as if the world were upside down
and we spend our day praying for resurrection

the clock dripping toward evening, my neighbour
clumsily strumming *House of the Rising Sun*
on his guitar, for hours, outside in the rain,
as I belt out the words in my head, *Oh mother,*
tell your children, not to do what I have done
stay where you are, don't walk, don't run,
this will only last a little while, and when
all this is over, I swear to god, things will change;
when all this is over, we will hang our heads in kindness
or in shame.

from **Very Far After**

so many words
wasted on
this gravid moon

sweeping dead leaves
by the hall door –
the wheel turning

four geese
then two –
twilight folding in

no frog
& no quiet pool –
this poor poem

fox
in the outside lane
– overtaken –

moss from the roof
softly falling –
the crows are up

in the breeze
the leaves –
rain without rain

Darling Buds

Out of dry twigs
the jut and peer
of green,

a 3D printer
extruding leaves
from patient trees,

pushing
sharpened blades
through still-dank earth,

snatching our breath
with its first
mad fling,

a cast of white
snagged on the blackthorn's
surreptitious spikes,

spiders' nightgowns
thrown out
to dry.

The Hungry Days

for Liam O'Callaghan

After a long summer's day,
alternatively swimming at the weir
and stretched out in the sun,
on empty stomachs
we face the long walk home.
Liam suggests we call
at the first likely house
and ask for bread.
To emphasise our hunger
we go into the front garden,
pull up handfuls of grass
and pretend to eat.
A woman comes out
and invites us in.
The smell of cooking
is overpowering,
we can't speak for salivating.
She leads us through the house,
quickly past the kitchen,
and out into the back garden.
'The grass is longer out here, boys,
help yourselves!'

Looking for Fungie

When the last boat turns to harbour, up
the throat of Dingle Bay, the search ends.
The motor sprays, white wake spreads, buoys
lurch, dip their heads to the empty sea.
Clouds, drifting on darkness, dim the day.
'He's gone dancing,' someone says to me.

Twilight was the time of your best show
since you never liked to see us go,
launching, flipping, a white belly flash,
falling back, a graceful splash, then up
again, arching silhouette between
lighthouse and the Reenbeg sea stack, as
if calling, 'Come back. It's not night yet.
No. Stay a while. I am not done playing.'

Time and tide. No matter how you tried
you couldn't stop the cold moon rising
over Beenbawn clifftops, as slow, old,
and stubborn as the Dagda, or stem
the flow that floods An Chois and swallows
Sláidín Beach to the wall twice daily,
rocks and all, just for fun, relentless
swell that drowned the King of Ulster's son.

We'd all agree that forty dolphin
years went by too fast. Now, as the last
watchers leave the shore in ones and twos,
spirits sore, sharing non-news from their
phones: 'Coming home. Can't do more.' Stars
appear, smudged in water. Alone, I
fear you've swum off into local lore
like Brendan, Mór, and *Ryan's Daughter.*

Three Haiku

lockdown
do the birds wonder
where we are?

green parakeet
the park chess players talk
about the rules

visiting
civil war trenches
summer grass

The Sea-Glass Cabinet

The gems are pinned and mounted,
now they call for names.
I could risk the sacrilege of
beryl or sapphire for these
diamonds in the rough, but
rather name them for the
wave-worn places.

Here's Oleron,
a shard of cobalt blue
warming at the foot of the citadel,
our faces brightening with the find.

Here's Carrigskeewaun,
its pale offering, a crystal droplet
of April sky, resting with coral and
sea-lettuce and our plodded prints.

And Keem,
whose amethyst rubs shoulders
with the glass of whalers,
their sunken bottles
now marbled trinkets
for seals and sand-eels.
They speck the sea with story
of whiskey, poison,
sackings and shipwrecks,
spilled tinctures,
stoppered letters
leached of unanswered ink.

Lost, they tumble
on the tongue of the tide
and, in the big lift,
toss fizzing secrets
into our waiting hands.

The Cats of St Catherine's

The cats of St Catherine's
Promenade along garage roofs,
Across work-from-home-shed-offices,
Along the corrugated,
The tiled,
The bricked,
The tarmacked.

I see the shape of them ebb and flow as they
Congregate,
Confer,
Then silently part ways,
Their white socks flashing
Against the dark.

Oscar Square Birthday Party

In the aftermath of a wintry spring
Cherry blossom confetti lines the streets
Tucked into the cracks of the gutters
Skittering across the road, under passing cars.

The children have gone home.
The streets have a cutlery-clink dinnertime hush
With air that smells like spuds on a roasting tray.
I breathe in the burn and the cook of it.

As a bloom of dark clouds begins to gather
Bleeding into a Victoria sponge sunset
And as a cake-scented breeze teases past,
Whispering, 'make a wish'.

Nettle

I'd like to bring my grandfather back to life just to get him stoned,
the good kind, the thirst and laughter kind. He had, I think,
    kind laughter.
My plan is this: I'd tell him the weed was nettle seeds I'd honed
to be smokeable, we'd use his pipe. *I hope twon't kill me*, he'd say,
    and me just after
dying. But I am his. People of his don't do him harm, we're
    reliable as clothing.
I'd watch him reinhabit his trout-skin, retake stock of his own mouth,
suck his false tooth like he used, laugh about this. I need to
    know some things.
Did being called Gaga put in or put out on him? Is it true that
    in this part of the south
they used to make known their love by whipping the object of it
    with a nettle?
True, Gaga would tell me, *the grasping of the stinger was the pain*
    that proved it.
Here he'd open his big bready hands and stroke out the lines
    where the leaves should settle.
Gentleness won't work. It should be in your hand before it knows
    you've moved it.
He'd fix his bloodshot eyes on Granny's mass card, curling on
    the shelf.
He'd tell me all of this. I wouldn't have to find out for myself.

The Geata Dearg

A hundred yards would be about from here to the Geata Dearg, or
She said she was at the Geata Dearg before it dawned on her

are shibboleths, but not ones so grand as 'shibboleth' intimates:
it's just shorthand, a little shop-talk that shopping here permits,

that for Dad is a means of exaggerating the nearness or farness
of a thing, for Pat Browne his field's entrance, for us a tennis

net during Wimbledon. We don't even know if the red in its name
is for its one-time paint or present rust, if it lacks colour or needs some,

but I've said it more often than most of my English.
I came out of this world, not into it.

Gúna mo Mháthar

Fo-amhrán thíos fúm
sa ghorm dhorcha, fé gloine
a leánn. Leá a scuabann uainn
na huile nasc idir chuimhne is an saol.

Gúna gormghlas mo mháthar
triailim orm é, é fuaite as snátha uiscí
a dhoirt an domhan isteach sa chuan.
Tá sé uaim ar feadh lae is oíche.

Fé thionchar na gealaí
imím go glé, mo chosa
ar strae, ar sileadh fúm i muirshiúl
amach thar mo dhoimhneacht féin.

Stoite ón dtír, luím siar
i seoithín seothó na farraige ciúine.
Titeann an spéir isteach im shúile.
Anocht beidh gach réalt ina seod.

Éistím leis an amhrán
na focail aduaine thar mo thuiscint
stractha óna chéile ag na cianta.
Braistint mar cheol ag éirí

ó níos faide siar ná m'fhoinsí
aníos ionam, i nguth séimh.
Céimeanna folamha, ceal brú
i gcoinne mo chos, mé lasmuigh

My Mother's Dress

There is an undertone of song
in the deep blue, under glass
that dissolves. Dissolves all
the ties of life and memory.

I try on my mother's indigo
dress, woven of water-threads
the world spilled into the harbour.
I need it for a night and a day.

Under the sway of the moon
I process in light, my feet
deviant, high-stepping me
far out beyond my depth.

Uplifted from land, I lie back
in the sea's gentle *seoithín seothó*.
The sky falls into my eyes.
Tonight every star will be a jewel.

I listen to the song
its words strange beyond understanding,
torn one from the other by time.
An impulse like music rising

from farther back than I know,
rising in me, its voice gentle.
Light steps, free of all pressure
against my legs, me outside

d'am is d'aimsir, b'eo liom trí
mhachairí méithe na mara, uiscí
an amhrais, foraois na feamnaí
áitreabh uisciúil na míolta mincí

na mbradán, na scadán, na bportán.
Na deilfeanna ag ráthaíocht i measc
smugairlí rón is anama na marbh,
guth síoda trí ghairdín an iascaire.

Luascaim mo lámha, d'fhonn uile
nóta a stiúradh suas. Tumaim
i dtreo dhordghuth na doimhne.
go dtí modarthacht is gruaim.

An bhfuil aon leigheas
ar na taomanna uile?
An mbraithfead an baol nuair
a bhuailfidh a speabhraídí í?

Nuair a chuirfidh sí uirthi
a cóta trom dubh? Nuair a
thiocfaidh an ollchraos uirthi?
Fanfad go foighneach léi

thíos anso
Fanfad leis an stróic
leis an súrac, le gluaiseacht
ghiorraisc, fuadar nó fotharaga

is i suasghluaiseacht amháin
bead ar an dtráigh
in uisce éadomhain gan eireaball
cead anála fachta.

of time, of seasons, away with me
through rich pastures of the sea,
waters of uncertainty, forests of seaweed,
briny habitations of minke whales,

of salmon, of herring, of crabs,
of dolphins gambolling in the midst
of jellyfish and the souls of the dead,
a husky voice in the fisherman's garden.

I wave my hands, to guide each and
every last note upwards. I plunge
towards the *basso profundo* of the deep
towards murkiness, towards gloom.

Is there an antidote
to all of the seizures?
Will I sense the danger when
she is gripped by her madness?

When she decides to don
her heavy black coat? When
the ravening comes over her?
I will endure and soothe her

down in these depths.
I will endure the rending,
endure the swallowing, the twist
and turn, endure tug and tumble

and with one swift upthrust
I will land on the beach
in shallow water, tailless,
knowing I can breathe.

Translated by Paddy Bushe

Clutharú

Siúlann sí ar a barraicíní
chomh héadrom agus is féidir.
Ní theastaíonn uaithi na taibhsí a dhíbirt.

Cén siosarnach é sin? Cén chogarnaíl?
Ná himigí, a deir sí. Freagraíonn
macalla a coiscéimeanna féin í.

Siúlann sí ó sheomra go seomra.
Leagann sí lámh ar gach log
ins gach adhairt.

Cuimlíonn gach ceann acu go cúramach.
Beannaíonn do na manta aoibhiúla
sna frámaí ar fud na mballaí.

Beannaíonn cuid acu ar ais.
Fearann sí fíorchaoin fáilte
roimh chomhluadar na dtaibhsí.

Cocooning

She walks on tippy toes as lightly as she can. She doesn't want to
scare the ghosts away. // What's that? Is that a whisper? *Don't go*,
she says. Only the echo of her footsteps replies. // She walks from
room to room. Touches the hollow in every pillow as she goes. //
She strokes each one with care. Salutes the gaping smiles that
hang on every wall. // Some smile, salute her back. With open
arms she craves the company of ghosts.

Legacy

Into the silver time capsule we placed
all the things that might be needed
to be understood: segments of the Milky Way,
white winter roses in bloom,
the four seasons, then added the sun,
moon and westerly wind, the cry of rooks
in the high wood. We mixed everything
with snatches of tunes, fragments of music,
the sound of wind in trees, traces of clouds
moving in a breeze, the dance language
of bees and added some books for good measure.

We included the run of a mill race, a mantilla
of delicate black lace, a whiff of sulphur,
all we could imagine that would let
whoever found it floating in space understand
our need to make ourselves whole again,
after we had cut down our treasure of forests,
poisoned the very air and emptied the seas.
We were not the meek.
Forgive us please.

Sean Scully Room, Dublin City Gallery

As a child how often had he been told
to keep between the lines yet here he is
leaving a blurry trail where red encroaches

on blue, yellow on black, white on grey,
where talk meets chat, bird and birdsong improvise,
stone builds on uneven stone. He shares notes

on how it's done – 'our Jack could do that' –
this first, then this, here open a different can, smell
the stain on the air though it's all as unsayable

as the sound of light posing for the artist who
taking up a brush like the indomitable child he is
paints it as something needing to be said.

The Winter Pony

The boy leans back in the two-wheeled trap,
  reins slipped between finger and thumb.

His pony trots, fetlocks high,
  the cobalt hooves are cracking along.

I imagine dizzying sparks that spit
  through the fog-drift as they speed

past Christmas-lit homes and trees,
  birch and oak a grey shimmer of stars,

branches splayed to fingerlets.
  The crack and whirr of hooves

and wheels recede, then silence falls.
  What remains is the long yawn back

to fallowness, this Monday morning's
  grey road, grey fields, grey house,

remote from summer's deep rustle,
  its tussled length of hours.

Only this: the small pony and boy
  now swallowed in time, a slow, iced air

breathing from the north,
  roots entwined in the dark earth.

SIMON Ó FAOLÁIN

Fásach

do Nuala Ní Dhómhnaill

'Gus in ainneoin gach a bhfuil agam,
De dheargainneoin saol na míne,
Tá an aisling thréan im' intinn.

Tá clochán in airde ar chliathán na Screige
– Díon fós ina sheasamh idir spéir agus talamh –
A dhéanfadh cúis.

Labhraíonn an fiach go bráthardha ann,
Ritheann giorria i gcoinne fána,
Dónn an fheadóg bhuí mar ghríos.

Ní bheadh iomairí pónairí agam ann,
(Tá's ag madraí an bhaile nach bhfásann
pónairí ar oileán ná ar shliabh gan fothain),

Mhairfinn ar fhraocháin, rútaí brioscláin, fuilig,
Agus b'fhéidir buidéal *Laphroaig*
I dtaisce in almóir an chlocháin.

Bheadh braon agam tráthnóntaí breátha,
Suite idir ursain an dorais ag féachaint
Ar ghrian na fola thar Shliabh an Iolair.

Do-scartha ó dheatach na móna sa bholgam
Bheadh blas na ndroichead dóite uilig,
Is ná chuirfeadh san aon mhairg orm.

132

Wilderness

for Nuala Ní Dhomhnaill

And in spite everything I have now,
Especially in spite of the easy life,
The vision still lives intensely within.

There's a beehive hut high on Screag
– Roofed still between earth and sky –
That would be enough.

Ravens speak fraternally there,
A hare runs uphill,
Golden plovers are incandescent.

I'd have no bean-row at all there
(It's common knowledge that beans
Don't grow on islands, or exposed mountains).

I'd live on fraughans, silverweed roots, chickweed,
And maybe a bottle of Laphroaig
Hoarded in a niche in the wall of the hut.

I'd have the odd drop on fine evenings,
Perched between the door-jambs watching
The sun set blood-red over Sliabh an Iolair.

Ingrained in the turf-smoke of every sip
Would be taste of all the bridges I burned,
And let that be no occasion for remorse.

Translated by Paddy Bushe

Teifeach

This is no world for escaped beings
To make their way back into
   — R.S. Thomas

Gur coimhthíoch thú anso ba léir,
Ach nuair a gheitis romham sa ród
Ba chosúil nach mbeadh aon teagmháil
Eadrainn ina eaclóg,
Le báine súile allta ag splancadh
Fé do ghlib rua le huamhan
Roimh an saol seo nó saol eile,
Sciorrais, chasais ag éalú
Ó chiapadh ag an Droichead Bán,
Ag tabhairt bóithrín ort a lúbann
Suas go bearna Mhullach Bhéil
Mar a rinceann aer fiain
Sa tsúil idir grua sléibhe
Agus mala liath néalta:
Duitse, seo tairseach na saoirse,
Lig do ghéim agus osclófar.

Seo mo ghuí duit, a *bhò Ghàidhleach:*
Go mbeidh an Féith Fia do d'fholach,
Go dteipe cuardach lucht an *Pet Farm*,
Go dté tú slán le hardchlár Bhréanainn
Mar raon siar go Más an Tiompáin
Is soir go Chathair Chon Raoi uainn,
Ach beir ar dhrom leat ualach éadrom
M'anama i measc na saor.

Refugee

That you are an outsider was obvious,
But when you shied from me on the road,
I knew that whatever might happen between us
Would be anything but an eclogue,
When the wild whites of your eyes flashed,
Under your russet fringe, in absolute
Terror of this or some other world.
You skidded, veering towards escape
From the harrying at An Droichead Bán,
Taking the bóithrín that twists and turns
Up towards the gap of Mullach Bhéil
Where some wildness in the air dances
Around the eye between the hill's cheekbone
And the grey eyebrow of cloud above.
Here, for you, is the threshold of freedom:
Your lowing there will grant you passage.

So here, Highland Cow, is my prayer for you:
May the magic cloak of *An Féith Fia* conceal you,
May the pet farm people fail to find you,
May you safely reach the high ground of Brandon
That you may range away west to Más an Tiompáin
Then eastward towards Cathair Chon Raoi,
Carrying on your back the airy burden
Of my own soul among the free.

Translated by Paddy Bushe

Lean-to

Hush of the hay shed where slices of light limit the rain
– It holds a thick quiet. I tell my partner this is where
I'll meditate, without candle or burning incense –
What dung-bound scent could be more worthy to offer
Than this once-field folded into flakes trussed with orange
Twine into bales stacked three high? Nourishing shelter
You are, a soft grotto, a grassy shrine without distraction.
The storm-fast river and jackdaws are unheard here. As children,
When we played sardines, that backward hide and seek, I would
Choose a closet shelved with out of season wool. The light
Wept in under the door. It was safe as our held breath.

If our seekers had been diverted,
How long would we have kept our silence?

WHEN SASKIA DANCED

My sorrow grows. It's not just that You left. But when You left my eyes went with You. Now, how will I cry? – Rumi

She began by swirling her long dark hair. Shoulders followed,
then hips, legs, feet until she was spinning, arms outstretched,
like a dervish around tent, room, field. I saw her dance
with a yellow scarf beside the gorse near Coumshingaun
Corrie Lake, like Cathy back with her lover under the waterfall
in Mahon Falls,

in a chalet with a circle of women, on the island of Skyros on
a cliff above the sea. She danced in a silk skirt from India
embroidered with gold, red, blue and silver threads, rippling
and spinning Greek light. Revolving around her heart in
a trance of bone, muscle, flesh. A mandala of coloured sand

carefully blown onto the surface by monks in orange robes, days
and days of spirals, curls, circles, flowers, leaves. Each time
her feet touched the ground she stamped one grain of sand,
day after day, the months of her life as she raised her son and
loved the men she loved. When Saskia danced the others
stopped to watch.

A rainy day we gathered in an open sided tent to dance for her
though none of us could dervish twirl to music she loved;
African drums, Bodhrans, Gipsy violins, Cymbals, Dumbek,
Pipes, Kirtans, Ave Maria as rain fell on the roof and on
the oak Michael said was strong enough to hold our grief.

A WALK AFTER BAD NEWS

if we had known how happy we were
when we were happy,
if we had marked our skin with it
so that it bruised the ambers of November,
would it have made a difference?

i ring off the long-distance call,
find my keys, and leave this house
with its obsessive silence pleading
for a wild noise from my throat.

the rain batters the roof of the car
and i drive to the river. soaked through
i walk the bankside and stop to watch
the moon nightswimming – her skin
on the water like solder dripping.

keys have fallen somewhere so i ditch
the car, walk home, and the rain stops
along the way. refrigerators hum
in locked-up bars. the trains are empty;
nose to wall. and in the long-distance
a bull, like a cello, lies in a field of snow.

Ballyvaston, Night

A night wind howls from dark seas;
Bridgeless expanses,
Hidden depths,
Along the longship-haunted lough –
Whipping violet-clotted clouds like weals
Across the surface of a waxing yellow moon.

These tides give shelter
To seven communities
In which brittle-stars
And sea urchins reign.

This sea is steeped in plutonium,
An unasked-for gift from the Cumbrian coast.
The coastal roads are empty now –
The sky overhead once filled with planes.

These waters are awash with dreams.

NESSA O'MAHONY

Liffeyside

Looked at from the north quays,
the roads to the south quays
are downhill streams to the river,
tumbling over their syllables –
Winetavern, Fishamble, Parliament.

Latitude Longitude

N50 30 13 *W9 27 38*

The swans have taken to the lake
left the shelter of bay for an island
Wood Island Rock – Cornamona Bay
Lough Corrib, exposed, with not a sign
of a wood, except for a few sally bushes
enough to trim the wind, curve gusts
away from a nest on the east side
in a hollow in the granite,
where grass grows
just tall enough
to protect
six eggs.

Others watch
from the tallest
branches of a stunted
ash – waiting for an opportunity
to dig black beaks into brittle shells
to drink the forming embryo into gullets
already lined with seagull albumen, thieved
from white-lichened rocks under screeching victims
nature as grey as the pair of hooded crows that wait
patiently, persistent assailants, nodding to each other.

Graveside Rain. May 2021

Happy is the corpse that's rained on
my mother says,
there was never a rain like it.
Torrential, cold, elemental.
The man dead was a farmer,
in the hospital thinking of a new tyre
for the tractor. His life a preservation
of the family history, the legacy. Roots.
There was never a rain like it.
Rain is good for growth, for the soil,
for life to spring again.
Life will spring again.
There was never a rain like it.
Torrential, cold, elemental.
We thought we'd never feel again
the heat in our bones.
Happy is the corpse that's rained on.
The man dead was a farmer
and it rained well
on the land that he loved.

Skellig Michael

A puffin is watching
the old monk fetching water
his back bent, neck burned
red from the sun. The surf
breaks against the boulders of cliffs,
monument of the forlorn, the monk
wipes the sweat off his forehead.
The bucket glistens
in the wet-green of an island
crumbling in the maelstrom of time,
the monk takes his breaths like breadcrumbs.
Along the brick wall he climbs
higher and higher up the stairs into
thin air. Clouds follow his progression,
a steady succession of steps,
like time suspended he transcends
into yesterday's blue.

Homage

to Louis MacNeice

The April sunlight in this churchyard
softens around the shadows it casts
on stones and souls who rest beside you.
I mean this with respect but I have come

because my intercontinental journey
proves you incorrect in saying poetry
is only 'surface vanity'. See how deep
I have plunged myself into foreign countryside –

ten hours on two flights, two hours on two
blue Ulster Buses, a thirty-minute uphill walk
through a winding, spectral neighbourhood,
through a living runway of swaying birches,

hearing every raven squawk, every leaf
tremble in the hushing spring wind,
to find Christ Church nestled, cosy
on top of a humble Carrowdore hill.

I am one from the hordes of faffing youth
indebted to debt itself, who still strive
for the title of Poet in this screened era,
who still think it important to sit before

a living-room-rug-sized patch of grass,
solitary and lacking daisies,
containing the lives of your granddad,
mother, sister, wife and you.

No matter the ninety years between our births,
or the fifty-eight passed since your departure;
the words you printed once upon a page
have braved oblivion, travelled time and farther.

O, Socks!

They'll recommend executives but I
despise the formal – elastic grips too high

along the calf. Striped crews prescribed by school
are knit from pins and Polyblend; not wool

a grandma weaves entwined with silk and lace
which hugs cold skin, creates a sacred space

for a foot to rest, forget where it has been,
in caramel embrace beside its twin.

Each heel deserves the softest of repose
upon a bed of candy floss. Your toes,

like babies cradled in their feather cots,
are sleeping in a sea of polka dots,

delicate as salted buttercream
melted into coffee, sweetening steam.

from **The Shoulder of Mutton Estate**

i

she came home some nights
and the house was gone,
so hanging her coat on a branch,
she grabbed a trowel
and set to laying blocks;

grey course after course she laid
till she stepped into the hallway,
the plasterboard walls she papered
then hall, stairs and landing
– the cornice was the tricky bit.

Then switching on the kettle
as the kids turned in their sleep,
the stars wheeling in the sky above,
she went out to the garden that had grown together again
and hung the washing on the line.

Fanacht

The mountains shift
in & out of cloud above the roofs

of the housing estate –
a surprise capping of snow

the day before Bealtaine, May Day.
Tides do their work, unseen –

the snow melts,
the moon thickens.

On the canal, a man in a caravan tells me
he's seen dolphins in the estuary,

the sleek rush of bodies in their element.
The swallows come back,

chitter on wires,
a kamikaze rally

of black & white shrieks,
wingbeats. I can feel

the disrupt of them
against my ankles,

they come so low;
refuse the garden's

sparse weediness,
its things in pots.

A swallow's heart
is less than the size

of a fingertip.
I could put one

in a pocket,
slip it under

my tongue,
tell no one.

I should be grateful
for this.

New Year Swim

Below the dunes at Culdaff they stand,
ready for dousing, the cleansing of sins.
Shoulders raised against the gale, they brace
to take the mantle of a year, twelve months
freshly minted, pure as silver.

In mottled hides of patchwork pink,
this herd of swearing bison
dredge solace from the heat
of nearby strangers, steaming
in the bellows of their breath.

The clock ticks on and roars rise up
from the belly of the crowd when a young bull
lowers his head, charges against the sea.
The rest stampede, move as human tide,
the thunder of a thousand feet on sand.

The ocean accepts it all, the sloughing
of jaded forms, the donning of new.
They lift themselves from this baptism,
raw as new-born calves,
dripping with aspiration.

Beauty

It can be small, quiet:
the hummingbird heartbeat of Aimée's fontanelle,
skeins of *kintsugi* gold in a lacquered rice bowl,
the purple-red chandeliers of roadside fuchsia.

I see it in spindly pavement cracks
radiating from the concrete starburst
around a street lamp.

In vast basilicas, I find it nestled
in the curlicues of acanthus leaves,
furled into baroque altar carvings.

These are my tiny totems, polished
as prayer beads, thumbed
when life becomes loud and ugly,
pushes into bladed focus.

Threads

xlii

Have a gander at my mother alone there at the table
threading the needle, steady-handed, yielding
to a flat-line motion. Watch how her eye levels,

how beads of sweat build with the heft
of what's before her – an elsewhere of light
flickering back through the hole in the steel.

She'll shed the clothes, step out of her own body,
and look back at the kitchen's isolation: damp spots
on the ceiling, cracks in linoleum, slips of pheasant-tail

wallpaper flapping. And now the kitchen succumbs
to *the music of what's happening;* the string of thread
licked and stiffened, a world beyond the eye.

NELL REGAN

A Letter

for Ilhan Çomak

I would send you
the horizon
folded in the crease
of this page. Now
a gesture of sea
that rushes
from it, now
the deep bow
of sky
toward it.
Home
resides in this
line between,
holding its
open gaze.

Overnight

Overnight the slight incline behind the house
became Máméan, walking it I could see
Croagh Patrick in the distance – a mound

of earth left by builders. A copse of trees
with its sprinkling of bluebells morphed into
Barna Woods, while an old ruin straddling

the boundary wall was Aughnanure Castle
or the remnants of a famine village depending
on my mood. Storms brought the Wild Atlantic

Way into the garden; barrels left out to catch
rainwater the nearest we got to Nafooey,
Lough Inagh – the day a frog leapt from one
I jumped for joy.

Mac Duagh's Well

O spring
inside the world,
forgive me
if I haven't
drunk my fill.

Tybroughney

When it seems as if it's all too broken
to mend, house flooding, house on fire,
there are these meadows by the river,
in winter a safe haven for wild swans.
'They eat more grass than I would like,'
says the farmer, 'but they need their place.'

All day the swans attend to that grass.
Neat scrolls of turd mark their progress.
Squabbles break out. No doubt
there are pecking orders, power struggles,
but lapwing and curlew drift in from the river,
feed close beside. There is room.

A bright field blessed for life is what
I might once have wanted to say.
If I come too close the swans straighten
and start to edge away. So I keep in
by the hedge and look on and button
by button my coat of shame is undone.

Reluctant Ascetic

smoke of Mt. Fuji
bends to the will of the wind
disappears on high
alas, my own wandering thoughts
where will they go, I wonder

deatach Shliabh Fuji
is sclábhaí na gaoithe é
imíonn as sa spéir
uch, mo chuid smaointe ar fán
cá ngabhfaidh siad in aon chor

and today once more
to the hill I'll make my way
where the pine winds blow
maybe come across my friend
as before, enjoying the shade

is arís inniu
raghaidh mé go dtí an cnoc
leoithne tríd an ngiúis
buailfead seans lem' chara ann
'bhí á fhuarú féin inné

as at them I gaze
I've grown very close indeed
to these blossoms all
parting with them when they fall –
such a bitter day 'twill be

nuair a fheicim iad
braithim an-chóngarach
do na blátha seo
titfidh siad go léir ar ball
och monuar nach trua an scéal

New transcreations in English and Irish of poems by tanka grandmaster and traveling acetic Saigyō (1118–1190), in which the original configuration of 5-7-5-7-7 syllables, associated with waka and tanka, is retained.

Kilbeggan Drive-In Movies

The Buicks, the Chevvies, Mustangs and Corvettes,
convertibles and hard tops, white walled, chrome plated,
first dates, blind dates, the couple, the betrothed
parked up in the church of American cinematography;
a throwback to the mid-west, mid-twentieth century,
popcorn, soda pop, hot dogs, coffee.

The stars shine from the giant screens
in black and white or technicolor. Dramatic scenes
where Bogart, Cagney, Garbo, Tracy or Hope
talk over the first kiss, the awkward grope.
The double leather seat, steering column gear shift,
space enough for love, be it slow, be it swift.

Fast forward to midlands Ireland, Covid-19.
A wet September night, the screen on a flatbed lorry –
Hulk, Iron Man and all the progeny of Stan Lee
fight to save the universe from the mythical reprobate.
The kids are filled with awe, excitement and all they can eat;
the parents, in each other's arms, doze off in the back seat.

Sparrow-hawk

Torn from
daydreams,
in front of
me on the
path, a young
sparrow hawk,
tawny white
plumage, corn yellow beak, its talons
gripping a bloodied pigeon, snagged in the
fence. He tries to fly, dragged down
by the weight
he will not
abandon. Our
eyes connect
momentarily,
uncertainly,
in parity

pfeilstörche

the word for a white stork
struck with an African arrow
drawing blood from a rotting wound
as it flies to its German home. i sit beside the window
with this new information;
a man passing by speaks in Bengali on his phone
(for a moment it felt like i belonged)
i wonder who it was on the other side –
is he talking to a lover
or with his octogenarian *nani*
squinting through her cataract? he's gone.
i make fresh coffee with roasted Kenyan beans
from O'Connell supermarket
of polite nods at safe distances vs.
probing questions from Pari *kaku* who sold me
instant coffee at the store in my old neighbourhood;
back at my window
dusty feet on cracked tar
497 miles towards home on a pastel Bengal road
teeth stained with raw tobacco & melting *gur*
human chain of visible spines
a class forgotten in a hurry
Pari *kaku* stares at me, unblinking, a dagger
between muscle & bone

Five Yeses of a Day and a Night

art after the downpour
the soft pottery selves
of worms

the horses gather …
a corner of the field
becomes the centre

a contrail unravels …
the hill keeps
its history

clearly invisible …
corners the bats turn
in flight

still climbing moonlight …
the spider's damaged
ladder

Maggie's Grave

On a day when the coast of Skerries looks like heaven
and those mountains that sweep down to the sea stand unclouded
I go looking for your name and find it on a hilltop
where the flowers are blown away
from the graves of village entertainers, widows of drowned sailors,
the fishermen who used to come back in the evening
with the silver of their catch.
Their days were all the same, a kind of misty rain
through which they saw the still world of a distant peninsula.
Their week was spent attentive to the sea
but anticipating Sunday on *terra firma*.
On a day when every shade of green looks greener,
when sea and headland appear God-given
I go looking for your name, climbing to a place
where those the healer could not save lie safe from the storms
    above them.

Cloud-watching in Roscommon

for Mary Cunningham

There is a landscape that might hold clues
to the beginning of time.
Its archaeology outwits the archaeologist
who pokes around in the rain-soaked sunshine.
When a day breaks with no shadow on the lakes
and the sky seems affable
we decide on a walk but before stepping out
clouds gather, the morning turns dark,
the wet hills become a vista half-vanished.
Up where the mines are closed a gale rises
like fits of laughter, the scenic routes are misty,
the pass impassable
and the ruins of antiquity are rattling.
The rain never stops. It takes us into a trance
repeating those rhythms it makes on stone walls,
the roadside shrines and Celtic cross.
We cloud-watch and wait for the drops to fall,
first a few, then the deluge that is unstoppable.

Boyle, June 2020

For the Year That's In It

I only know I have slept
because I have dreamt.
I only know I have dreamt
because the events occurred outside my house.

In month two, season one
of increased looking, decreased speed,
of what is immediate. One returns to
making a basket, small circles with the mind and hands.
Somewhere past an allowable distance
hawthorn froths, a hazel decks itself in catkins.

We are told to wear gloves if we must
touch anything outside our homes.

Lying on the grass between the cars and the road
to see how the ground feels.

In month three, season two
the plants I watch every day have grown.
The neighbour, seeing this, gives me all of her plants,
says I have a 'gift from God'. She is a nurse
but her plants are dying. She also gives me a box of latex gloves.

Parting the children from one another
outdoors when one shouts, 'Look what I found!'

Month four, what is found:
One dead wood pigeon.
A refashioning of the rules, we may now expose our hands.

Hand sanitizer, once scarce, now flows from gin distilleries.
What else is found:
A taste for gin.
For each botanical ingredient, the ability to picture the entire plant.
The car's ability to keep itself clean.

Priests in a Caravan (Small, Not Far Away)

Your tears on my shoulder on this cold October
morning could freeze,
small sheets of heartbreak upon my skin
from the clouds of your eyes.
The topic of long distance has only been touched
upon with cautious emotive withdrawal,
like tongs in hot oil or a net
into the tank of feeding piranhas.
My feigning of bravery: to make you laugh
I mimic that scene from *Father Ted*
where he uses the small toy cow to differentiate
between merely being small
and being far away.
Your laugh and my kiss on your temple tells us
that for now we have silenced this ghost of contempt –
until it rears its head again, all I can do
is love you with more than my heart so that
I might seem small and not far away.

Aristotle's Lantern

The centre of a sea urchin
is known as the Blessed Virgin.
So I was told in school: with help
I spotted her veiled aspect
in the meeting of the mouthparts.
But years later, searching for urchins –
shells frail as communion wafer –
you laughed and said, *Back home
the centre is called Aristotle's Lantern.*
And aren't we all lanterns drawing meat
to the red light of our mouths?
              Picking our way back
        over rills of sewage run-off
        on Sandymount Strand
        we found gulls dropping
        dog whelks. Shells smashed
        on the concrete path, gulls
        dug into the grey-pink mucous.
        One whelk whooshed past my ear,
        spun off my shoulder – *This
        is how Aristotle died*, I said,
        then realised it was Aeschylus,
        a vulture and a falling turtle.
        Close enough. I threw the shell
        back to the gulls – we watched
        the snatch, the fight. Our faces,
        upturned, felt brittle as the centres
        of urchins. As eager.

Senan's Church/*Teampall Seanáin*

1

pavement narrow as a kerbstone
                         padlocked black gate

]cling to its bars for balance
                         wedge into the gatepost

scan the hilly enclave   wall remnants   gravestones

traffic whirs by
             turn to see it spring from the bend
                                        descend
                                        river bound

2

follow the wall to a flight of steps
bring a key for the narrow gate
                         walk on his ground

a new cross and altar   rings of benches
                         troughs of flowers

debris in the nave space   laths and crates
                         shoved in a corner of his ground

walk out to its vantage points   scan for the river

rest at the yew trunk
that curves to clear a gravestone

                          turns vertical
                          where its branches sprout

Fields

Is there anything to forgive
when two ageing cats curl
and stretch on the deck at sundown?
Their moulting fur
brings laughter to mind
as little white wisps mingle
with the stems of cornflowers.

Forget the drained cups and glasses,
the blue plastic sunscreen bottle.
Remember the fields beyond tall trees
where evening light is striking now.
Glance furtively at the stone Buddha
whose hand touches the earth.

A Caravan In The Rain

for Matthew Cordner

How delicious to fade away to the pachinko melody
    of rain
that wipes clean the scoreboard and erases the day's zero sum game,
    a migraine
    lifting,
    a heatwave
    giving way
so we can slip into the snowy centre of a ball of wool
    and filtrate
our corporeal weight through the drumming of hundreds of digits,
    these waves
of fluid paradiddles that invite us – warm, safe, unanchored –
    to break
through the confines of this cruel and unsparing cosmos … to let go
    of the reins.

Wren

Cave dweller, King o' Birds, here you sit, brazen,
perched atop a gravestone in the full sun

among the fading foxgloves, where Blake is laid and Bunyan
your tail sticking up – an exclamation mark! –

your chest puffed out
singing your complicated note.

Little troglodyte, little tree-creeper,
here is an old woman, here an office worker

and here is someone from the hospital
nursing a wounded eye.

In this old plague-ground, on this hill of bones
see them unwrap themselves, settle to eat,

trailing their plague-masks, their bandages,
gulping their coffees and sandwiches,

inhaling the pestilent air,
happy to see a wren singing there.

How nicely you hold your tiny skeleton!
How nicely you mirror theirs, sternum, clavicle!

How short is a wren's life. Barely two years.

Lughnasa

I did not know you back then, when I dived
into Dillon's *Connemara Lovers,*
moonlight bathing Inishlacken, over
couples and the incoming sea. I've lived
beneath its gentle gaze, watched many tides
rise and fall like my hopes through nights flooding
with pastel tones, a sense of what's missing.
Waiting for a signal on Skype, I find

my mind stops and cycles back to the night
we first danced to *Nuvole Bianche*
in your kitchen, with your arms snugly tucked
in the small of my back. August moon bright
on Belfast brick, the harvest light fading
when all was locking down, and we were opening up.

Hanging Washing

On a fine day
when I hang clothes,
I feel that I am drying myself
under the sun
after being washed
utterly clean.

Tossed about by the soapy water,
rinsed well
wrung out
creases stretched
then on the line
under the sun.

Flies and butterflies come to bask
for a moment.
I'm inside out,
stark naked.

Pinched a little
by the pegs.

Mother

Her hair is tangled bladderwrack
and her skin the cockled flagstone
and her hands a map of the underworld
and her fingers pitchforks in potato beds
and her arms a bare glacial trough
littered with sediment left behind by her children
and her cheeks two puddles of chalk dust
and her words branches of the oak tree
and her train of thought a bog road
and her stories bees swarming
garden to garden, impossible to follow
and her laugh a monsoon shower
and her feet two carpenters' planes
sliding along floorboards in slippers
and her cough a cuckoo's call
and her regrets swallowed milk teeth
and her anger a circus bear swiping at nothing
and her smile a bridge between countries
and her hospitality a pine copse, evergreen
and her home a tapestry she has woven
with all the grasses and wildflowers
of the hillside, her Mount Olympus.

Trampoline

Where she'd once leaped, spun, looped
and flopped, hair and arms
akimbo, Tinsley now sits slow
as a Buddha or mendicant, her eyes
strained to pandemic laptop at school
on her giant trampoline, shade
cast by pin oaks and hardy maples,
air cut by the first fall breezes
blown hither from Kansas and Colorado.

Tinsley at work brings calm and balm
to my pandemic heart. Ms. Hays
calls out from locked-down Avery Elementary,
her hands guide lessons, float Powerpoints
from schoolhouse to Tinsley's trampoline.

It's her mind's motion, her heart's attention,
the wind's cool aspiration that rocks,
though gently, this pre-teen's trampoline.

It's September so Missouri's dry
and warm. Tinsley's learning though
she's escaped from school. She's
seated on a trampoline, she's placed
her laptop on her knees, her red hair
moving on the breeze. Remember,
sad compatriots, school's first day:
somnambulating Millpark Rd., metre
by sour metre as heat was sucked
from morning, hope evaporated

from tender hearts. Is it Mathematics
my neighbour ponders or some topic
that hits my liking button more:
The Battle of Gettysburg or Custer
beaten at The Little Big Horn? Two metres
is mantra for this pandemic but three cheers
for Tinsley absorbing all, seated on her trampoline.

Window

This starling, not in the wave but this precise one, this kind bird, with tiny beak you barely see, this starling, not in a murmuration, where the flow outdoes the particular, but in the dot, the black dot that moves in the centre, fine mark in a hollowed sky,

with twists and un-flying un-burdened movement, this bird who understands the whole, starling whose point is a beak, this one true bird in a single movement, in a line, followed by her brethren,

who starts the order of things, pre-empts the beginning, pre-curser to the thought, but freeing along the bay, along the cord of day that strings in single lines, that leaves wide sky in her wake,

who understands her sky better than her brethren, this starling, who like the first star beguiles the watcher on the rye, the gatherer of nothings,

singer in the black specks of others, birding in the truth of flighting, bird who cannot be seconded, who breathes sky and light will not catch her this pre-empting, hovering quiver, silent reed becoming the end – you never saw as she was grace-gone, she never listened to you,

never once actually moved her wing to propel her first she never inched her sweet wing, never caught a friction in air, the high up wind, she swallowed the space, was swallowed too but wings were bent back and motionless she moved without shaking

or sideways movement, she listened to nothing but the breeze at her back not once did she twitch to recognise her side and not one feather out of place.

Quarantine

i.m. Eavan Boland

From the frying pan and hopefully not into the fire
we travelled six thousand miles and at Addis Ababa
saw queues for China and people dressed as astronauts
hermetically sealed for the journey home, back to the epicentre
which had already shifted direction toward ours.

Perhaps ill-advisedly, we sipped beer in the 'London Bar'
and watched it all pass when our daughter welled up
at the whole incongruity of it all, spacesuits passing
in front of us and screens to the right and left of us,
streaming horror headlines.

My lights being heavy we exchanged the *cordon sanitaire*
of our compound, the veranda, heat and high altitude of Harare
for the loan of a gate-lodge on your family farm – built in Black '47
but more Wordsworthian now in its yellow wash and waiting wisteria.
A spell in rural rectitude and cold comfort Ireland but the beacon

of home strengthening. The clocks obligingly went back the weekend
of our arrival, but dawns are grey and the lengthening evenings
hold no heat. I hog the fire and the cold outside is freighted with fear,
blood thinned by a near decade in the tropics. The demesne trees
are towering spectres of leaflessness and up on the hill,

the only colour in rows of planted ash is the flicker of gold
in the wing of a finch. I look down upon a great quilt of fields
and even the land has taken on a verboten feel,
I might as well be staring upon the ice sheets of Antarctica.

Apartment

In the apartment between apartments, on the stairs, by the
landing, a door, a handle turning into the apartment, a shadow,
a figure, a head turning outside the window of the apartment,
across the street from the apartment, a car, stops, engine running
outside the apartment, a coffee cup shakes on the dashboard
below the apartment, a passerby ducks under the awning of
the apartment as the rain comes down, a sea gull circles above
the apartment, and a train on the bridge glimpses itself in the
reflection of the windows of the apartment, in the apartment, the
apartment is outside the apartment on the street of the apartment,
everyone splashes through the puddle of the apartment, walks
along the halls of the apartment, through the walls of the
apartment, between the apartment, on the stairs, on the landing,
bodies rushing into themselves,

After

in memory Janet Mullarney, 1952 – 2020

After her death, the artist rises
from the kitchen floor, surveys

the indigo bird she's cut in lino there,
wipes her hands on a cloth and sees

from her window that Spring has come,
is a patch of park with cherry blossoms.

Then her peacock struts through her hall,
flapping out into the stilled world

ahead into time to here, where we stand now
at her house with the narrow white door,

on the gate our candle flickering upright
in yellow memory. The dead artist

watches all this – how we walk back
through the dark, the streets subdued.

There's a cat, white on a shabby wall.
Cranes reach their long arms high up

to the moon's pink aura. All of this
she sees, minutes after she dies.

And how, in Newmarket Square, graffiti
startles on night's billboard: *Try Poetry.*

CHRIS AGEE was born in California and now lives in Belfast. His latest books are *Blue Sandbar Moon* and *Trump Rant.*

JAMES ANTHONY was born in Athlone in 1969. His most recent publication is in Voxgalvia, *Galway Advertiser,* 2020.

IVY BANNISTER was born in NYC. Her essay 'Dublin Made Me a Writer' appeared in *Look! It's a Woman Writer!* (Arlen House, 2021).

STEPHEN BEECHINOR (Cork, Ireland, 1974) recently translated Juan Rulfo's *El Llano en llamas* (Structo Press, 2019) from Mexican Spanish.

LINDSEY BELLOSA was born in Syracuse NY but now lives on Clare Island in County Mayo.

TRISH BENNETT hails from the Leitrim/Fermanagh border. Her micro-pamphlet, *Borderlines,* was published by Hedgehog Press (2019).

CLÍODHNA BHREATNACH was born in Waterford City in 1992. Her most recent publication is in *Banshee,* Issue 12 (Autumn, 2021).

DENISE BLAKE was born in Ohio in 1958. Her latest collection is *Invocation* (Revival Press). She is a regular contributor to RTE's *Sunday Miscellany.*

DERMOT BOLGER is a Dublin-born poet, novelist and playwright. His eleventh poetry collection, *Other People's Lives,* will appear in 2022.

FIÓNA BOLGER was born in 1972. She lives between Ireland and India. Her next collection is due out from Salmon Poetry in 2022.

CAROLINE BRACKEN was born in Clonmel, Co. Tipperary and lives in Dublin. Recently published in *The Best New British And Irish Poets 2019-2021* (Eyewear Publishing).

ELLEN BRICKLEY was born in Dublin in 1984. Her most recent publication is in *Banshee,* Issue 10 (Autumn, 2020).

CAT BROGAN was born in Omagh, Tyrone. Tedx speaker, MA Writer/Teacher, shortlisted for NW Words, published in *The Golden Shovel.*

PADDY BUSHE was born in Dublin in 1948 and now lives in Waterville, Co. Kerry. His latest publication is the dual-language *Double Vision* (Dedalus Press, 2020)

DAVID BUTLER is a Bray-based poet and novelist. His latest poetry collection is *Liffey Sequence* (Doire Press, 2021).

DARAGH BYRNE grew up in County Kildare and has lived on Gadigal land in Sydney for the last twelve years.

SARAH BYRNE was born in Cork in 1984. Her most recent publication is in *The Irish Times* (November 2020).

ALVY CARRAGHER was born in Galway in 1989. Her most recent publication is *the men I keep under my bed* (2021).

PAUL CASEY was born in Cork, Ireland in 1968. His collection *Virtual Tides* was published by Salmon Poetry in 2016.

JANE CLARKE was born in Co. Roscommon in 1961. Her most recent publication is *When the Tree Falls* (Bloodaxe Books, 2019).

SUSAN CONNOLLY was born in Drogheda in 1956. *Bridge of the Ford* (Shearsman, 2016) is her tribute to her home town.

POLINA COSGRAVE was born in Volgograd, Russia in 1988. Her most recent publication is *My Name Is* (Dedalus Press, 2020).

CATHERINE ANN CULLEN was born in Drogheda in 1961. She is the inaugural Poet in Residence at Poetry Ireland and an award-winning poet, songwriter and children's writer.

MARTINA DALTON was born in Waterford in 1963, and lives in Tramore. She was awarded a Dedalus Press mentorship in 2021.

PHILIP DAVISON lives in Dublin. A novelist and playwright, his most recent book is *Quiet City* (Liberties Press). He is a member of Aosdána.

CELIA DE FRÉINE was born in Newtownards 1948. Her latest book is *I bhFreagairt ar Rilke: In Response to Rilke.*

EILÍN DE PAOR lives in Glasnevin. Her debut pamphlet, *In the Jitterfritz of Neon,* co-author Damien B. Donnelly, is in press.

PATRICK DEELEY is from Loughrea and has long lived in Dublin. *The End of the World* is his most recent collection of poems from Dedalus Press.

MICHELLE DENNEHY was born in Dublin. Her work appears in current editions of *Abridged, Honest Ulsterman* and *Bangor Literary Journal.*

MOYRA DONALDSON was born in Co Down in 1956. Her most recent publication is *Bone House* (Doire Press, 2021)

DARREN DONOHUE is from Newbridge, Co. Kildare. His debut poetry collection titled *Secret Poets* will be published by Turas Press in April 2022.

MICHAEL DOOLEY was born in Limerick in 1986. His poems appear in a variety of literary publications, mostly in Ireland.

MARGUERITE DOYLE is from Dublin. She holds an MA in Creative Writing from DCU and has studied Russian at TCD.

GER DUFFY lives in Co Waterford. She received a Mentoring Award in Poetry from The MlC in 2021.

TIM DWYER was born in Brooklyn in 1956. He lives in Bangor, Co. Down. His chapbook is *Smithy of our Longings* (Lapwing Publications, 2015).

LORETTA FAHY, born in Sligo, currently lives in Brussels. She has been published in *The Irish Times* 'New Irish Writing' and in *An Capall Dorcha*.

CIAN FERRITER was born in Dublin in 1969. He has lived most of his adult life in the Glasnevin area.

AGNIESZKA FILIPEK was born in Lower Silesia, Poland, in 1982. Recently her work has appeared in *Lucent Dreaming Magazine*.

JAMES FINNEGAN was born in Dublin. Publications include *Half-Open Door* (Eyewear Publishing, 2018) and *The Weather-Beaten Scarecrow* (Doire Press, forthcoming in 2022).

MARIA FITZGERALD was born in Co. Tipperary. She writes about identity, motherhood, love and loss and our interactions with nature and place.

KIT FRYATT was born in Iran in 1978. His most recent book of poems is *Bodyservant* (Shearsman, 2018).

CATHERINE GANDER was born in England and lives in Ireland. She has work forthcoming with Nine Pens Press's 9 Series.

ELAINE GASTON is from the North Antrim coast. Her collection is *The Lie of the Land* (Doire Press, 2015).

MATTHEW GEDEN lives in Kinsale, County Cork. His most recent book is *The Place Inside* (Dedalus Press, 2012).

ANGELA GRAHAM was born in Belfast in 1957. Her most recent publication is the short story collection, *A City Burning* (2020).

KEVIN GRAHAM was born in Co. Dublin in 1981. He recently published a pamphlet with Ragpicker Poetry called *First Impressions*.

MARK GRANIER was born in London in 1957. His most recent collection is *Ghostlight: New & Selected Poems* (Salmon, 2017). He lives in Bray, Co Wicklow.

CLAIRE HENNESSY was born in Dublin in 1986. She is the author of several YA novels.

KEVIN HIGGINS was born in London in 1967. He grew up in Galway City where he still lives. His fifth collection will be published in 2022.

CATHERINE HIGGINS-MOORE is from Hillsborough, County Down. Her chapbook *Strange Roof* was published by Finishing Line Press. She has recently been published in *Poetry London* and *TLS*.

MARY-JANE HOLMES spent her childhood in Antrim. Her most recent publication is *Set a Crow to Catch a Crow* (2021).

LIZ HOUCHIN was born in Rathfarnham, Dublin in 1973. Her first chapbook will be published by Southword in December 2021.

Born in Congo, NITHY KASA was raised in Kinshasa and Galway. Her work was added to the UCD Library Special Collections in 2021.

BEN KEATINGE was born in Dublin in 1973. He is editor of Making Integral: Critical Essays on Richard Murphy (2019).

PATRICK KEHOE lives in Enniscorthy, Co. Wexford. The most recent of his three collections of poems is *Places to Sleep* (Salmon Poetry, 2018).

Poet, novelist and broadcaster JOHN KELLY's first collection of poems, *Notions,* was published by Dedalus Press in 2018. A second collection, *Space,* will be published in 2022.

ÖZGECAN KESICI was born in Munich to Kazakh-Turkish parents and holds a PhD in Sociology from UCD. After spending a substantial part of her adult life in Dublin, she now lives in Berlin.

CLAIRE-LISE KIEFFER, born in France in 1990, lives in Galway. Her poem 'Peony Picker' was shortlisted for the Fish Poetry Prize.

BRIAN KIRK was born in Dublin in 1964. His most recent publication is *After The Fall* (Salmon Poetry, 2017).

ZOSIA KUCZYŃSKA was born in Solihull in 1988. Her most recent publication is *With others in your absence* (Emma Press, 2021).

EITHNE LANNON is a Dublin-born poet. Her first collection, *Earth Music,* was published in 2019 by Turas Press.

NOELLE LYNSKEY lives in Portumna, Co. Galway. Her work is published in many anthologies and literary magazines.

CATHERINE PHIL MACCARTHY grew up in Co. Limerick and lives in Dublin. Her most recent collection is *Daughters of the House* (Dedalus Press, 2019).

JIM MAGUIRE was born in Enniscorthy in 1962. His book Music Field was shortlisted for the Shine/Strong Award in 2014.

KATIE MARTIN, born in 1975, grew up in Tallaght, Dublin. She has recently completed her first poetry chapbook.

JAKI MCCARRICK was born in London. Her award-winning writing has been published by Samuel French, Routledge, Aurora Metro and Seren Books.

DEIRDRE McMAHON, born in Dublin (1957), is a literary translator, working from German, whose work has appeared in journals and online.

MEL McMAHON was born in Lurgan, County Armagh, in 1968. His latest book, *Beneath Our Feet,* was published in 2018.

MARIA McMANUS was born in Enniskillen, 1964. Her most recent collection is *Available Light* (Arlen House, 2017). She lives in Belfast.

WINIFRED McNULTY is from Leitrim and Leicester, and now lives in Donegal. Her work most recently appeared in Southword.

JOHN MEE lives in Cork. He won the Patrick Kavanagh Award in 2015 and the Fool for Poetry International Chapbook Competition in 2016.

PAULA MEEHAN was born in 1955 in Dublin where she still lives. From 2013–2016 she was Ireland Professor of Poetry. Her selected poems, *As If By Magic,* was published by Dedalus Press in 2020.

VICTORIA (VIKA) MELKOVSKA was born in Ukraine in 1977 and lives in Dublin. Poems feature in *Writing Home* (Dedalus Press, 2019).

KELLY MICHELS was born in Chicago and moved to Dublin in 2019. Her most recent pamphlet is *Disquiet* (Jacar Press, 2015).

BILLY MILLS was born Dublin in 1954 and lives in Limerick. He is co-editor of hardPressed Poetry. His most recent collection is *The City Itself* (2017).

GERALDINE MITCHELL was born in Dublin. Her most recent publication is *Mute/Unmute* (Arlen House, 2020).

GERRY MURPHY is an Irish poet, born in Cork in 1952. His latest collection is *The Humours of Nothingness* (Dedalus Press, 2020).

KIERAN FIONN MURPHY, born in New York in 1966, lives in Dingle and is studying writing (MA candidate) at UCC.

TIM MURPHY was born in Cork in 1967. He lives in Madrid.

DENISE NAGLE, a Mayo-based writer, was born in 1974. Her poems have been published in national and international journals.

CHANDRIKA NARAYANAN-MOHAN is a Dublin-based writer from India. Her work has been published by *Poetry Ireland Review,* UCD Press and *Banshee,* among others.

File Gaeilge í CEAITÍ NÍ BHEILDIÚIN a bhfuil gradaim buaite aici. Is as Baile Átha Cliath ó dhúchas do Cheaití atá anois ina cónaí ar Leithinis Chorca Dhuibhne. CEAITÍ NÍ BHEILDIÚIN is a prize-winning Irish language poet, originally from Dublin and now living on the Dingle Peninsula.

DAVID NASH was born in Cork in 1985. His most recent publication is the pamphlet *In Case of Death* (2015).

ÁINE NÍ GHLINN, poet/children's writer was born in Co Tipperary in 1955. Her most recent collection is *Rúin Oscailte* (2021).

JEAN O'BRIEN was born and lives in Dublin. She has five previous collections. Her latest, *Stars Burn Regardless,* is due shortly.

HUGH O'DONNELL, born in Dublin, 1951. *Time to Call Home,* reflections on the natural world, was published by Veritas in 2021.

MARY O'DONNELL has lived in Kildare since 1977. Her eighth collection, *Massacre of the Birds,* was published by Salmon in 2020.

SIMON Ó FAOLÁIN was born in Dublin and raised in the Corca Dhuibhne Gaeltacht, Co Kerry. His latest collection is *Fé Sholas Luaineach* (Coiscéim, 2014).

JAMIE O'HALLORAN was born on Long Island, New York in 1955. Her poems appear in *One Hand Clapping* and *Crannóg.*

LANI O'HANLON was born in Dublin and is living in West Waterford. She is a dance artist/therapist and writer.

EUGENE O'HARE was born in Newry in 1980. He was shortlisted for the Belfast Book Festival poetry prize, 2021.

MAEVE O'LYNN was born in Belfast in 1984. Her most recent poem published in Epoch Press's journal (Summer 2021).

NESSA O'MAHONY was born in Dublin. Her most recent publication is *The Hollow Woman on the Island* (Salmon Poetry, 2019)

ART Ó SÚILLEABHÁIN was born in Corr na Móna, Co Galway in 1956. His most recent publication is *Mayflies in the Heather* (2021)

MAIRÉAD O'SULLIVAN was born in Killarney in 1993. Her ethnographic piece 'Roots' appeared in the *Irish Journal of Anthropology* (July, 2020).

ANDREAS PARGGER was born in Austria in 1986. His most recent publication is in the anthology *Jahrbuch der Lyrik* (2019).

SAAKSHI PATEL was raised in Bombay, India in 1997. Her poems most recently appeared in *yolk* (2020).

KEITH PAYNE was born in Dublin in 1975. John Broderick Writer in Residence 2021. Co-editor of *A Different Eden: Ecopoetry from Ireland and Galicia* (Dedalus Press, 2021).

KATE QUIGLEY was born in Meath & lives in the west of Ireland. Their first pamphlet, *If You Love Something,* was published by Rack Press in 2019.

RUTH QUINLAN is originally from Kerry but now lives in Galway. She is co-editor of *Skylight 47,* a bi-annual poetry magazine.

CLIFTON REDMOND was born in Hacketstown and lives in Carlow. He has recently had work published in *The Cormorant Anthology.*

NELL REGAN was born in London in 1969 and lives in Dublin. Her latest collection is *A Gap in the Clouds,* a co-translation with James Hadley (Dedalus Press, 2021).

Dubliner MOYA RODDY has lived for almost 30 years in Galway. Her poetry has been shortlisted for the Hennessy and Strong/Shine Awards.

MARK ROPER was born in Swanwick, England, in 1951. His most recent publication *Bindweed* (Dedalus Press, 2017).

GABRIEL ROSENSTOCK was born in Kilfinane, Co. Limerick in 1949. He is a poet, tankaist, playwright, haikuist, novelist, essayist, and author/translator of over 180 books, mostly in Irish.

JOHN SAUNDERS was born in Wexford in 1956. His last collection, *Chance*, was published in 2013.

COLM SCULLY was born in Cork in 1966. His poems have most recently appeared in *Cyphers* and *Crannóg* magazines.

From India, SREE SEN is based out of Dublin and Westport. Her most recent publication was a poem in *The Honest Ulsterman*.

JOHN W. SEXTON was born in London in 1958. His most recent collection is *Visions at Templeglantine* (Revival Press, 2020).

GERARD SMYTH was born in Dublin in 1951. His most recent collection is *The Sundays of Eternity* (Dedalus Press, 2020).

KERRI SONNENBERG, b. 1974, is from Chicago, USA. She is author of *The Mudra* (2004). She lives in Cork.

LEAH TAYLOR was born in Belfast, Northern Ireland in 1997 and is a recent poetry master's graduate from Queen's University.

ROSAMUND TAYLOR was born in Dún Laoghaire in 1989. Her work appears in *Queering the Green: Post–2000 Queer Irish Poetry.*

BETTY THOMPSON was born in Dublin in 1951. Her most recent publication is in *Cyphers*, Issue 92 (2021).

ROSS THOMPSON lives, and teaches English, in Bangor, Co. Down. *Threading the Light,* his debut collection, was published in 2019.

RÓISÍN TIERNEY was born in Dublin in 1963. She lives in London. *Dream Endings* won the 2012 Michael Marks Pamphlet Award. Her latest pamphlet is *Mock-Orange* (Rack Press, 2019).

EOGHAN TOTTEN was born in London in 1993. He is a Michael Longley scholar studying poetry at Queen's University Belfast.

ERIKO TSUGAWA-MADDEN, Japanese, has lived 30 years in Dublin. Her bilingual poetry book, *Lull in the rain,* was published in 2021.

NIAMH TWOMEY was born in London in 1995. Her work most recently featured in 'New Irish Writing'.

EAMONN WALL was born in Co. Wexford in 1955. His most recent book is *From Oven Lane to Sun Prairie: In Search of Irish America* (Arlen House, 2019).

CHRISTIAN WETHERED was born in Pembury, England. He was most recently published in *The Madrigal.*

JOSEPH WOODS recently returned to Ireland after eight years in Burma and Zimbabwe. His *Monsoon Diary* was published by Dedalus Press in 2018.

ADAM WYETH was born in England and lives in Dublin. His latest publication, *about:blank,* is published by Salmon Poetry (October 2021).

ENDA WYLEY was born in Dublin, 1966. She has published six collections of poetry and is a member of Aosdána.

≈

ABOUT THE EDITOR

PAT BORAN was born in Portlaoise and has long since lived in Dublin where he has worked as writer-in-residence, festival organiser and radio broadcaster. The editor of more than 100 anthologies and individual collections, he is the author of a dozen collections of his own poetry and prose, most recently the poetry books *The Statues of Emo Court* (2020), *Then Again* (2019), *A Man is Only as Good: A Pocket Selected Poems* (2017) and *Waveforms: Bull Island Haiku* (2015), the latter the subject of a recent radio documentary. Editions of his poetry have been published in many languages, including Georgian, Greek, French, Portuguese, Italian, Macedonian and Hungarian. He is a member of Aosdána, the affiliation of creative artists in Ireland, and the recipient of a number of poetry awards including the Patrick Kavanagh Award and the Lawrence O'Shaughnessy Award. Since early 2020 much of his work has been in the medium of poetry film, with his films being selected for festivals in Ireland, the UK, the US, India and elsewhere. His films, as well as poemcards and samples of his published books, may be found at his website at *www.patboran.com.*

Acknowledgements and thanks are due to the editors and publishers of the following in which a number of the poems collected here originally appeared:

Dermot Bolger: a film version of 'Eden Terrace' (film by Daniel Sedgwick with sound by Mark Lynch) appeared on the RTÉ website (10 July 2021); Pat Boran: the poet's film version of 'Building the Ark' has been shown at a number of festivals, including *Irish Film from Home,* London, the *Shine Online International Film Festival,* Toronto, the *New York Flash Film Festival, Make Art Not Fear,* Porto, Portugal and the *Nature and Culture Poetry Film Festival,* in Copenhagen; David Butler: 'Light Rail' appeared in *Liffey Sequence* (Doire Press, 2021), and is reproduced here by kind permission; Daragh Byrne: 'Bronte After Lunch' appeared in *Westerly* (July 2021); Jane Clarke: 'First Earlies' appeared on the WRITE where we are NOW blog (Manchester Metropolitan University), April 2020, and was also broadcast on *The Poetry Programme,* RTÉ Radio 1, June 2020; Catherine Ann Cullen: an earlier draft of 'Shell House Folly, Bushy Park' appeared on the *Placing Poems* poetry map at https://placingpoems.com/ for Poetry Day Ireland 2021; Philip Davison: 'Station Man' appeared in *Stepaway Magazine,* Issue 32; Loretta Fahy: 'City Sparrow' appeared in 'An Irish Garland', a series of short productions shared by the Irish Embassy Belgium via their Twitter page, December 2020; Catherine Gander: 'The Comfort of Mallards' appeared as part of a number of postcards for the Poetry Ireland 'Poetry Town' initiative, September 2021; Mark Granier: 'The End, Etc.' appeared in *The Honest Ulsterman* (October 2020); Brian Kirk: 'Planting' was written as part of a sequence of formal poems responding to life during the Covid-19 pandemic and was made with support from the Arts Council of Ireland / An

Chomhairle Ealaíon's Covid-19 Response Award. It appeared in *Live Encounters Poetry,* December 2020, and in a short film by Martha Kirk on YouTube, June 2020; Jim Maguire: 'Frederick May in Clontarf' appeared in *Poetry Salzburg Review,* Issue 37, Summer 2021); Katie Martin: 'Our Statues Go Unwatched' appeared in *The Irish Times,* July 2020; Kelly Michels: 'Lockdown' originally appeared in Poetry Ireland Review; Kieran Fionn Murphy: 'Looking for Fungie' appeared in *West Kerry Live,* November 2020; Tim Murphy: 'lockdown' appeared in *Frogpond,* Issue 43:2, Spring/Summer 2020, 'green parakeet' appeared in *Presence,* Issue 69, March 2021, 'visiting' appeared in *Autumn Moon Haiku Journal,* Issue 4:2, Spring/Summer 2021; Jamie O'Halloran: 'Lean-to' appeared in T*he Night Heron Barks* (Spring 2021); Lani O'Hanlon: 'When Saskia Danced' was originally commissioned by Dominic Campbell, Arts and Cultural Engagement, The Irish Hospice Foundation, for an in-house poetry pamphlet, 2021; Ruth Quinlan: 'Beauty' appeared in *Abridged,* Issue 0–68, Trivia issue, March/April 2021; Leah Taylor: 'Priests in a Caravan (Small, Not Far Away)' appeared in *Spellbinder* (Autumn 2021)

Finally, a huge thank you to Aoife Lynch for her invaluable editorial assistance and calm head under pressure during the making of this anthology.

Lightning Source UK Ltd.
Milton Keynes UK
UKHW012011261021
392889UK00002B/54